Alcohol

Other Books of Related Interest

Teen Decisions Series
Pregnancy
Sex
Smoking
Violence

Opposing Viewpoints Series
Addiction
Alcohol
Chemical Dependency
Drug Abuse
Opposing Viewpoints in Social Issues
Teens at Risk
The War on Drugs

Current Controversies Series
Alcoholism
Illegal Drugs
Teen Addiction

Contemporary Issues Companions Series
Drunk Driving

At Issue Series
Heroin
Marijuana

Alcohol

William Dudley, *Book Editor*

David L. Bender, *Publisher*
Bruno Leone, *Executive Editor*
Bonnie Szumski, *Editorial Director*
Stuart B. Miller, *Managing Editor*
James D. Torr, *Series Editor*

Greenhaven Press Inc., San Diego, California

Library of Congress Cataloging-in-Publication Data

Alcohol / William Dudley, book editor.
     p. cm. — (Teen decisions)
    Includes bibliographical references and index.
    ISBN 0-7377-0489-6 (pbk. : alk. paper) —
    ISBN 0-7377-0490-X (lib. : alk. paper)
    1. Teenagers—Alcohol use. 2. Drinking of alcoholic beverages.
3. Alcoholism. I. Dudley, William, 1964–   . II. Series.

HV5135 .A3858 2001
362.292'0835—dc21
                                   00-057828
                                      CIP

Cover photo: © The Stock Market

© 2001 by Greenhaven Press, Inc.
PO Box 289009, San Diego, CA 92198-9009

Printed in the U.S.A.

Contents

Foreword

The teen years are a time of transition from childhood to adulthood. By age 13, most teenagers have started the process of physical growth and sexual maturation that enables them to produce children of their own. In the United States and other industrialized nations, teens who have entered or completed puberty are still children in the eyes of the law. They remain the responsibility of their parents or guardians and are not expected to make major decisions themselves. In most of the United States, eighteen is the age of legal adulthood. However, in some states, the age of majority is nineteen, and some legal restrictions on adult activities, such as drinking alcohol, extend until age twenty-one.

This prolonged period between the onset of puberty and the achieving of legal adulthood is not just a matter of hormonal and physical change, but a learning process as well. Teens must learn to cope with influences outside the immediate family. For many teens, friends or peer groups become the basis for many of their opinions and actions. In addition, teens are influenced by TV shows, advertising, and music.

The *Teen Decisions* series aims at helping teens make responsible choices. Each book provides readers with thought-provoking advice and information from a variety of perspectives. Most of the articles in these anthologies were originally written for, and in many cases by, teens. Some of the essays focus on ethical and moral dilemmas, while others present pertinent legal and scientific information. Many of the articles tell personal stories about decisions teens have made and how their lives were affected.

One special feature of this series is the "Points of Contention," in which specially paired articles present directly opposing views on controversial topics. Additional features in each book include a listing of organizations to contact for more information, as well as a bibliography to aid readers interested in more information. The *Teen Decisions* series strives to include both trustworthy information and multiple opinions on topics important to teens, while respecting the role teens play in making their own choices.

Introduction

Alcoholic beverages are popular in American culture and are readily available to many teens. Alcohol is also a cause of 100,000 deaths every year in the United States, according to the National Center for Health Statistics (most deaths are through alcohol-related car accidents and homicides in addition to health problems such as cirrhosis of the liver). Because of alcohol's potential harms, all fifty states in the United States have made it illegal for people under 21 to purchase alcoholic beverages. But most teens, despite these laws, will probably have many opportunities to drink. The choice of whether and how to consume alcohol is ultimately a personal one. The combination of alcohol's popularity, its potential harms, and its illicit status for teens makes this choice one of the more important and difficult decisions teens make as they navigate through adolescence.

Alcohol and Teens

Alcohol (also called ethyl alcohol or ethanol) is a colorless, inflammable liquid chemically composed of carbon, oxygen, and hydrogen. By itself, alcohol has a strong burning taste that dries out the mouth and throat, which is why it is almost always consumed in greatly diluted form. Beer generally contains between 3 to 6 percent alcohol, wine is usually 10 to 14 percent alcohol, and distilled or "hard liquor" such as whisky and gin ranges from 40 to 70 percent alcohol. A can of beer, a glass of wine, and a shot of whiskey all contain about .6 ounces of alcohol. Alcohol is a powerful substance—a drug—that even in small amounts can have strong effects on a person's body, mind, and emotions. This accounts for its popularity. It also accounts for many problems.

Humans have consumed alcoholic beverages of some sort or other since prehistoric times. In contemporary American society alcohol is commonly served at social and family gatherings and at bars and restaurants. Approximately two-thirds of American adults drink to some extent. The manufacture and sale of alcoholic beverages is a large and influential industry that sponsors numerous sporting and entertainment events and advertises heavily to promote its product by associating it with fun, success, and popularity.

Alcohol's popularity in the United States extends to teens. Researchers have estimated that as many as 4 million adolescents consume alcohol in any given month—and that the average age of first alcohol experimentation is 12. The University of Michigan's Monitoring the Future Study, an annual survey of underage drinking, has consistently found that a significant portion of teens have tried alcohol. In 1997, for instance, 24.5 percent of eighth graders, 40 percent of tenth graders, and almost 53 percent of high school seniors reported drinking alcohol the previous month.

However, alcohol also marks one of the clearest demarcations in American society between adults and minors: While adults can legally purchase and consume alcohol, it is illegal in all fifty states for people under 21 to purchase alcoholic beverages or to possess or consume them in public settings. The legal technicalities vary by state, and you probably won't be arrested for sipping champagne at a wedding toast. But in most cases, if you choose to drink alcohol and you are under 21, you are breaking the law.

Many teenagers might view this as unfair. If alcohol is so accepted, why is it illegal? Why are teens forbidden to do something that is legal and popular for adults? What's the big deal? Briefly put, alcohol is a potentially dangerous substance that can easily be abused, and can inflict physical, emotional, and even (some would argue) spiritual damage on individuals who abuse it. To consume alcohol without harm requires mature and responsible decisions about drinking, something not all teens—or adults—practice.

Adults are not immune from the risks of alcohol abuse—in fact, most teen alcohol problems also befall adults. And whether prohibiting teens from drinking is the best way to prevent teen alcohol abuse is a matter of debate. However, teens can be especially vulnerable to some of the problems alcohol can create through its short- and long-term effects on the body, mind, and behavior.

Blood Alcohol Content and Intoxication

When a person drinks an alcoholic beverage, be it a beer, wine cooler, or something else, alcohol is absorbed through the mouth, stomach, and small intestine into the bloodstream. The body's liver can break down or metabolize alcohol at a steady rate (about an ounce per hour for an average-sized adult). When a person consumes alcohol faster than the liver can break it down, alcohol accumulates in the blood and the person becomes intoxicated—in other words, drunk.

The physical symptoms of intoxication depend on the individual and on the amount of alcohol concentrated in the blood. This is expressed as a person's blood alcohol content or concentration (BAC). A BAC of .05 indicates that the blood contains .05 percent alcohol. A BAC of .10 means that alcohol makes up one tenth of one percent of a person's blood (or one part alcohol per thousand parts blood). This is the legal level of intoxication in most states.

A person weighing 160 pounds would generally need to consume five drinks over the course of one hour to attain a BAC of .10 (a drink being one 12 ounce beer, 5 ounce glass of wine, or 1½ ounces of 80 proof liquor). However, the amount of alcohol it takes to reach a certain BAC level is hard to predict for individuals. Body chemistry differences cause women to often experience higher BACs than men consuming the same amount of alcohol. Blood alcohol levels may also rise quicker for inexperienced drinkers or those especially sensitive to alcohol. Children and teenagers, whose nervous systems aren't as developed as adults and who are generally smaller than adults (and thus have smaller total amount of circulating blood) are more vulnerable to the intoxicating effects of alcohol. Teens typically can become "drunk" faster and with less alcohol than adults.

Teens also often become drunk because of how they drink alcohol. Intoxication can be prevented or moderated by some simple steps, such as limiting one's alcoholic beverage input, drinking slowly, and consuming alcohol with meals (food in the stomach slows alcohol absorption). Thus, sipping a glass of wine with dinner is unlikely to result in significant intoxication. However, many teens in the United States instead frequently drink large amounts of alcohol in a short period of time. They have less experience in judging how intoxicated they are and are more prone to make reckless decisions. In the University of Michigan survey previously cited, 8 percent of eighth graders, 22 percent of tenth graders, and 34 percent of seniors reported getting drunk over the previous month. The Office of Juvenile Justice and Delinquency Prevention reported in 1996 that 9.5 million U.S. teenagers admitted to drinking alcoholic beverages; of which 40 percent admitted to "binge" drinking (drinking five or more drinks at a single setting), which is more than enough to become intoxicated. Young adults between the ages of 18 and 25 are statistically the most likely to be binge drinkers.

Alcohol's Short-Term Effects on the Body and Brain

Alcohol, especially when consumed in a "binge" drinking fashion, has significant short-term effects on both teen and adult drinkers. Alcohol's interference with digestion in the small intestine may cause diarrhea. Alcohol can swell and close the pyloric valve—the opening between the stomach and small intestine—and cause vomiting. Alcohol's effects also include the conglomeration of unpleasant symptoms—headaches, nausea, dry mouth, and dizziness—known as the hangover. Hangovers are actually forms of alcohol withdrawal caused by, among other things, a water imbalance in the body.

The body organ most affected by alcohol is the brain. Alcohol is a depressant that suppresses the production of brain chemicals called neurotransmitters. This works to slow down the functions of the brain and the nervous system. Among its noted effects are "blackouts" or loss of memory and decreased mental sharpness and judgment. The changes alcohol enacts on the brain can be greatly multiplied if it is consumed with medicines or other drugs.

As a drinker's BAC increases, so does alcohol's effects. Part of what the brain does is control impulses and emotions. Thus at BACs of .01 to .04, a person may feel a decrease in inhibitions and a sense of elation or relaxation. At .05 or .07, the drinker's alertness is diminished and feelings of anxiety and depression may be increased. Vision and reaction time can also be affected. At .10, signs of intoxication include clumsiness, loss of balance, and slurred speech. A person with a BAC between 0.15 and 0.20 may stumble around, insist he or she is not drunk, explode in a rage, and not remember anything later. Emotions—fear, anger, joy—may become uncontrollable. Consciousness is lost at somewhere between 0.30 and 0.40. Alcohol can cause death at concentrations of 0.40 and above as the brain areas controlling the heart and lungs fail to function. Bradley McCue, a University of Michigan student, drank twenty-four shots of liquor in less than two hours to celebrate his 21st birthday. An autopsy revealed a BAC of 0.44.

Consequences of Impaired Judgment

Although death by alcohol poisoning is relatively rare, alcohol's impairment of the brain and its functions can lead to many problems ranging from trivial to fatal. Intoxication may simply lead to embarrassing incidents of stupidity. But it may also lead to unplanned sexual encounters that could result in unwanted pregnancies or acquiring HIV/AIDS or other diseases. Alcohol use is implicated in the majority of "date" rape cases among teens and college students. The alcohol-induced shedding of inhibitions and judgment may cause people to engage in fights or criminal activities. A 1987 study of youths held in juvenile detention halls revealed that nearly a third of them were under the influence of alcohol when they were arrested.

One place where alcohol's dulling effects on the brain can be especially deadly is behind the wheel of a car. In 1996, 17,126 Americans were killed in accidents in which alcohol played a role. Laws exist that make driving while intoxicated a serious offense. Drunk driving risks and laws apply to both adults and youth, but a teen's driving inexperience and alcohol can make for an especially deadly combination. Automotive mishaps involving drunk drivers are the leading cause of death for people between the ages of 15 and 24.

Chronic Effects of Heavy Alcohol Consumption

The long-term risks of alcohol abuse are just as grave as immediate ones for both teens and adults. Alcohol can have significant long-term ramifications for health. While some studies have suggested that moderate alcohol consumption can prevent heart disease, long-term effects of consistent and heavy alcohol consumption include damage to the liver and pancreas, cancer, malnutrition, and stroke. In men alcohol can decrease testosterone production and cause impotence, while pregnant women who drink heavily may give their children physical and mental birth defects—a condition called fetal alcohol syndrome (FAS). In addition to health impairments, heavy alcohol use among both adults and teens can result in trouble with the law, shattered friendships and family difficulties, and problems in school and the workplace.

stess

Why Do People Drink?

Why do some people continue to consume alcohol even though it might be harming their body or getting them in trouble with the law? Much as alcohol affects both adults and teens in both similar and different ways, teens both share some of the same motivations for drinking as adults and have reasons of their own. Drinking for the wrong reasons can lead to the problem of alcoholism.

A 1995 study found that 66.7 percent of teens surveyed said they use alcohol and other drugs to help them forget their problems. All teenagers face different sorts of pressures and problems as they go through puberty or enter middle and high school. They are struggling to establish independence from family. Teens worry about their appearance, dating, and sex. Some teens worry about belonging to the right "crowd," while others have trouble making friends. Some may be stressed about grades in school and going to the right college. Others focus on making money in the workplace for themselves or their families. Some teens face pressure to join gangs. Many teenagers go through arguments and struggles with their parents; some teenagers come from families that are dysfunctional or abusive.

While the circumstances of teens differ from adults, many of the underlying pressures are similar. Adolescence is characterized in part by the intrusion of adult pressures and concerns into teen lives. Teens—and adults—are both continually faced with the challenges of deciding who they are, ascertaining what values are important to them, finding spiritual meaning in their lives, conforming with social expectations, finding a satisfactory vocation, and seeking rewarding human relationships including marriage and family. For many, alcohol can be a way of escaping the pressures they face and the dissatisfaction they feel about life. The problem is that alcohol often becomes a trap. It can make you feel better, but it doesn't solve any underlying problems. Those who go to alcohol as a crutch often soon resort to drinking on a regular basis just to cope with things.

Alcoholism

People who use alcohol this way are at extremely high risk for alcoholism. Alcoholics are people of all ages and situations who drink because they are dependent on the drug. They feel compelled to drink even if their drinking has caused significant problems in school, employment, and relationships. The National Institute of Alcohol Abuse and Alcoholism has estimated that almost 14 million people have alcohol problems, of which 8.1 million are alcoholics or alcohol addicts. Alcoholism in the past has been viewed as a problem that strikes only adults. However, researchers now estimate that almost 4 million teens in the United States have an alcohol addiction problem.

Alcoholism is characterized by a strong compulsion to drink, inability to stop drinking, physical withdrawal symptoms from alcohol such as nausea, shakiness, and anxiety, and the buildup of tolerance for alcohol making more alcohol necessary to get drunk. Alcoholism often runs in families. Some suspect it may have a genetic component—some individuals might be biologically more susceptible to developing an overpowering craving for alcohol if they drink.

Studies have found that teens who start drinking before age 15 are four times more likely to become alcoholics later in life than teens who abstain until age 21. Those who get intoxicated to boost their self-esteem or to escape their problems are at the greatest risk. Leah's story is fairly typical. "When I wasn't wasted," she told a writer for *Teen Magazine*, " I felt bored, lonely, and depressed. I thought I was ugly. I didn't fit in with anyone." Drinking made her feel "more mature." Leah drank every day by the time she was a freshman in high school and dropped out in the middle of her sophomore year. "I couldn't have a good time unless I was wasted." Like many alcoholics, Leah went through a period of denial in refusing to recognize she had a problem (drunks were "old men who begged for quarters on the street," not young people like herself). Eventually she admitted she had a problem and entered a group therapy program for teens. Therapy groups such as those sponsored by Alcoholics Anonymous constitute the most popular method of treating alcoholism in the United States. But alcoholism, most believe, can be treated but not cured; one is always a "recovering alcoholic."

Deciding About Alcohol

The risks of alcoholism are one of several factors you should consider when making decisions about this popular substance that enriches the lives of many but destroys the lives of others. Moreover, these decisions do not go away when you reach the magic age of 21. The risks associated with alcohol do not vanish. Adults still become alcoholics or problem drinkers if they are not careful. Drinking and driving still do not mix. Alcohol will still give you hangovers—or worse—if abused. Deciding about alcohol is a lifetime process.

The selections in this volume, many written by teenagers or people recounting their teen experiences, are aimed to enrich your understanding of some of the consequences of consuming alcohol. Chapter One, What Is Alcohol and How Can It Affect You? provides factual articles and personal anecdotes on the effects of alcohol. The articles in Chapter Two, Alcoholism and Problem Drinking, include information on organizations and treatment options for people who suspect they may be addicted to alcohol (see also the listing of organizations and websites at the end of the book). Chapter Three, Alcohol, Driving, and the Law features graphic personal stories of teens who have survived alcohol-related accidents and information on some of the laws states have enacted to control the problem of drunk driving. Chapter Four, When Someone You Know Has a Drinking Problem, is directed at the many teens whose lives are touched by alcohol—not through their own drinking, but by the drinking of friends and family members. Chapter Five, Deciding About Alcohol, concludes this volume by returning to the question

facing you and other teens: What should you do about this popular substance that, for the time being at least, is legally prohib-
ited? Teens and others examine such matters as responding to
peer pressure and how one can say "no" to a drink if offered.

To drink or not to drink? The choice is ultimately yours. *Teen
Decisions: Alcohol,* is not meant to provide all the answers or to
make the decision for you. But it is hoped that the information
provided here will help make your decision a responsible one.

What Is Alcohol and How Can It Affect You?

Teen
Decisions

The Facts About Alcohol and Teens

KidsHealth.org

The following article by a children's health center gives you the facts about what happens to your body when you drink. It provides some basic information on the chemical ethyl alcohol and what it does when it enters the bloodstream, and why it can cause problems for many people. The article also tells you some steps you can take to avoid drinking or to seek treatment if you think you have a problem with drinking. KidsHealth.org is the award-winning website of the Nemours Foundation Center for Children's Health Media.

Just about everyone knows that the legal drinking age throughout the United States is 21. But did you know that the average American has his or her first drink around age 13? According to the National Institute on Drug Abuse, 82% of high school seniors have used alcohol. In an average month, about 9.5 million American teens drink alcohol.

Teens who drink put themselves at risk for many problems—problems with the law, at school, and with their parents just to name a few. Deciding whether to drink is a personal decision that we each eventually have to make. This article provides the facts about alcohol and teens, including how alcohol affects your body, so you can make an educated choice.

What Is Alcohol?

Alcohol is created when fruits, vegetables, or grains are *fermented,* that is, when a microorganism—like yeast or bacteria—causes sugars in the original item to change into alcohol. Fermentation is used to produce many necessary items, such as cheese, penicillin, B-complex vitamins, and citric acid. Even alcohol is a useful product; it can be used as a solvent, an antiseptic, or a sedative.

> Deciding whether to drink is a personal decision that we each eventually have to make.

So if alcohol is a natural product, why do teens need to be concerned about drinking it? When people drink, alcohol is absorbed into their bloodstream. From there, it affects the central nervous system (the brain and spinal cord), which controls virtually all body functions. Alcohol is a *depressant,* which means it slows the function of the central nervous system. That's why drinking small amounts of alcohol reduces anxiety. Alcohol actually blocks some of the messages trying to get to the brain. This alters your perceptions, your emotions, and even your vision and hearing.

More alcohol causes greater changes in the brain, resulting in

---

The Amount of Alcohol in One Drink
- 12 ounces of beer (5% alcohol)
- 5 ounces of wine (12% alcohol)
- 1.5 ounces of liquor (40% alcohol)

Each of the three types of alcohol listed above has about the same amount of ethyl alcohol—.6 ounces.

National Clearinghouse for Alcohol and Drug Information

intoxication. People who have overused alcohol may stagger, lose their coordination, and slur their speech. They will probably be confused and disoriented. Intoxication can make people very friendly and talkative or very aggressive and belligerent. Reaction times are slowed dramatically.

When large amounts of alcohol are consumed in a short period of time, *alcohol poisoning* can result. Alcohol poisoning is very dangerous. Violent vomiting is usually the first symptom, as the body tries to rid itself of the alcohol. Extreme sleepiness, unconsciousness, difficulty breathing, and even death may result.

Why Do Teens Drink?

For starters, people drink and use other drugs to feel good. Experimentation with alcohol during the teen years is common. Some reasons that teens use alcohol and other drugs are:
- curiosity
- it feels good
- to reduce stress and relax
- to fit in
- to feel older

From a very young age, kids are bombarded with advertising messages depicting beautiful, hip young adults enjoying life— and alcohol. This glamorous portrayal of alcohol may not be geared toward teens and kids, but it can still affect them. Plus, many parents and other adults use alcohol socially, having wine with dinner, for example. In this setting, alcohol seems harmless enough, so many teens may think, "Why not?"

Why Shouldn't I Drink?

Even though it is illegal to drink alcohol in the United States until you are 21, most teens can get access to alcohol, or will at least be exposed to it or have friends who drink. It is therefore up to you to make a decision whether to drink.

Deciding to drink while a teen can have many harmful consequences. Some occur right away, and others build up over long periods of time. Consider that the average teen first tries alcohol around age 13. This is long before the body or mind is ready to handle a powerful drug like alcohol. And the earlier kids start drinking, the more likely they will be to develop a problem with alcohol or drugs later in life.

> Deciding to drink while a teen can have many harmful consequences.

Many teens think that drinking alcohol will help them to relax and feel cool. Actually, drinking often makes people do stupid things. You may end up feeling embarrassed. Drinking also gives you bad breath, and having a hangover is the pits. It's sort of like having the flu: pounding headache, intense thirst, nausea, extreme sensitivity to light and noise, blurry vision, shakiness, exhaustion, and more. Ugh!

Different Reactions to Alcohol

Every person is affected differently by alcohol. Some people can drink an enormous amount without seeming to be affected by it. Others are affected by half a can of beer. Some people's livers are extremely sensitive, so that after years of "moderate" drinking, they discover that they've developed cirrhosis of the liver and protest, "But I've never even been drunk." Some people quickly develop a dependence on alcohol almost from the moment of their first drink; other people may drink "casually" for months or years, then wake up one day to realize they've become highly dependent on alcohol.

Elizabeth A. Ryan, *Straight Talk About Drugs and Alcohol*, New York: FactsOnFile.

Drinking can really damage your ability to perform well at school and sports. Many parents disapprove of their teen's drinking and punishment often results. Teens who drink are more likely to be sexually active and to have unsafe, unprotected sex. Resulting pregnancies and sexually transmitted diseases can change—or even end—lives.

Some teens drink because they think it will help them escape from other problems. Although this may seem like a good idea, drinking always leads to even bigger problems. Teens who drink are more likely to get into fights and commit other crimes. This increases your chance of having legal problems or going to prison. In fact, research shows that 32% of teens under 18 who are in long-term juvenile detention centers were under the influence of alcohol at the time of their crime and/or arrest.

Teens who drink may get seriously hurt or even die. Over 38% of all drowning deaths are alcohol-related. Use of alcohol greatly increases the chance that a teen will be involved in a car accident, homicide, or suicide.

> Alcohol can take a lot of the enjoyment out of your teen years.

Long-term alcohol use can have extremely serious health consequences. Liver damage is a widely known consequence of alcohol abuse. Years of drinking can also damage the pancreas, heart, and brain. Heavy drinking can lead to malnutrition (if alcohol is used as a substitute for food) or obesity (if regular or binge eating is combined with the high calorie content of alcoholic beverages).

How Can I Avoid Drinking?

Let's face it: if all your friends drink, it may be hard for you to say "no thanks." Not doing what many others do can be hard, especially for teens whose friends are really important to them. No one wants to risk feeling rejected or different.

If saying no to alcohol makes you feel uncomfortable, one effective strategy is to blame your parents or another adult for your refusal. Saying, "My parents are coming to pick me up soon," or "I already got in major trouble for drinking once, I can't do it again," can make saying no a little bit easier.

You can also make sure that you and your friends have plans to do something besides just hanging out in someone's basement drinking beer. Plan a trip to the movies, the mall, a concert, or a sports event—anything that gets you out of the house. You might also organize your friends into a volleyball, bowling, or softball team—any activity that gets you moving.

Where Can I Get Help?

When a teenager realizes that she has a drinking problem, she needs to get help as soon as possible. Contacting a caring adolescent doctor or school guidance counselor for advice is usually a good first step. They can refer students to a drug and alcohol counselor for evaluation and treatment. In some states, this treatment is completely confidential. After assessing a teen's problem, a counselor may recommend a brief stay in rehab or outpatient treatment. In recovery, a teen's physical and psychological dependence on alcohol will gradually be overcome.

What to Do If You're Concerned About Someone Else's Drinking

Many teens live in homes where a parent or other family member drinks too much. This may make you angry, scared, and depressed. It's important to realize that many people can't control their drinking without help. This doesn't mean that they love or care about you any less. Alcoholism does not make people bad, it just means that they have an illness that needs to be treated.

Here are some common signs that a person has a problem with alcohol:
- using alcohol to escape problems
- major changes in personality when drinking
- high tolerance level for alcohol (he or she needs to drink a lot more to get "high")
- blackouts (not remembering what happened when drinking)

- problems at work or school because of drinking (like missing work or performing poorly)
- inability to control drinking (can't set limits and stick to them)

People with drinking problems can't stop drinking until they are ready to admit they have a problem and get help. This can leave family members and loved ones feeling helpless. The good news is there are many places to turn for help. An adult whom you trust, such as your guidance counselor, can refer you to a professional or group who can help.

If you have a friend whose drinking concerns you, make sure she is safe. Don't let anyone drink and drive. *Ever.* If you can, try to keep friends who have been drinking from doing anything dangerous, such as trying to walk home at night alone or starting a fight.

Try to remember all the fun stuff you can do with your time instead of drinking. You can play sports, go out with your friends, learn new hobbies, work to earn extra spending money, go shopping, see movies, and dance, just to name a few. You can enjoy your teenage years without alcohol. And alcohol can take a lot of the enjoyment out of your teen years.

The Symptoms of Alcohol Poisoning

Mayo Foundation for Medical Education and Research

Alcohol is a poison. Some forms of alcohol, such as those found in antifreeze, kill a person who ingests a small amount. But the ethanol in alcoholic beverages can be just as fatal if a person drinks a large amount over a small period of time, or takes it along with other drugs or medications. A physician at the Mayo Clinic briefly describes some of the symptoms of acute alcohol poisoning.

The symptoms of poisoning or intoxication from alcohol depend on the type of alcohol.

The effect of ethanol (ethyl alcohol or grain alcohol), contained in alcoholic beverages, is related to its blood level. Factors such as the amount consumed, the concentration of alcohol in the drink, the time over which it is consumed, and the presence of food in the stomach affect blood levels. The effects of acute ethanol intoxication cover a spectrum from giddiness and uninhibited behavior to slurred speech, muscular incoordination, incoherence, coma and even death. In addition, chronic use of ethanol can damage many parts of the body including the brain, nerves, heart muscle and liver. The damage done to vital organs by long-term alcohol abuse also may lead to death.

Reprinted from "Ask the Mayo Physician," by Mayo Clinic Health Oasis (www.mayohealth.org). Reprinted with permission from the Mayo Foundation for Medical Education and Research, Rochester, MN 55905.

Other forms of alcohol not intended for human consumption may produce toxic effects specific to the type of alcohol. Methanol (methyl alcohol or wood alcohol) is used commercially as antifreeze and as a solvent in some paint and varnish. It is very toxic if ingested—as little as a few swallows could prove fatal. Its effects include headache, cramps, convulsions and depressed breathing. In addition, methanol can damage the optic nerves and cause permanent blindness.

Ethylene glycol is another alcohol found in antifreeze for motor vehicles and in lacquers. It has effects similar to ethanol but also can cause kidney failure and death. Isopropyl rubbing alcohol also is toxic and can cause incoordination, stomach irritation, depressed breathing and coma.

> The effects of acute ethanol intoxication cover a spectrum from giddiness and uninhibited behavior to slurred speech, muscular incoordination, incoherence, coma and even death.

Perhaps the most important point to remember is that all forms of alcohol are toxic to some degree. Those not intended for human consumption may quickly cause death following ingestion. Ethanol, too, can be fatal in excess or if taken in combination with other central nervous system depressants such as sedatives, tranquilizers, and some pain medications and anticonvulsant medications. In addition, accidents related to alcohol abuse take thousands of lives each year.

Alcohol Poisoning Almost Killed Me

Kimberly Reardon

Can people actually die from drinking too much? In the following story, a teenager tells her account of how drinking led her to spend a scary night at the hospital emergency room. Alcohol nearly killed Kimberly Reardon when she passed out and stopped breathing after a party. Reardon is a high school student and correspondent for *Buffalo News*.

A fter hearing about Scott Krueger, the college student who died from drinking [at a September 1997 fraternity party], I decided it is my turn to speak up. I had a very similar experience when I was only 13, but I was lucky enough to be saved.

A little more than a year ago [in 1996], I was partying with my friends. I always drank alcohol on the weekends, and sometimes during the week. But on this Friday night, I drank more than normal. I drank almost a full bottle of Goldschlager, a strong liquor. Obviously, I don't remember much about the whole night.

I woke up in Lockport Memorial Hospital in the intensive care unit around 3 A.M. My parents and the doctors and nurses were by my side to tell me what happened.

They said that all the friends I was with knew I was extreme-

Reprinted from Kimberly Reardon, "A True Story of How Alcohol Can Kill," *The Buffalo News*, November 11, 1997. Reprinted with permission from the author.

ly drunk, but were too scared to call 911 or get help of any kind. So they just drank more themselves and didn't do anything. But luckily, a miracle happened. The baseball game my parents went to was rained out. They came home to find no one home, where I was supposed to be. They decided to go look and see if I was down the road.

They found me unconscious, with one of my friends trying to load me onto a three-wheeler. My dad ran back to the house and called 911. A few ambulances and police cars came. In the ambulance, I went into cardiac arrest. They revived me and stayed with me until we arrived at the hospital. Once we arrived there the nurses pumped my stomach to relieve me of all the poison from the alcohol.

For a while I couldn't breathe, because my mind couldn't tell me to breathe. So I was hooked up to a machine that breathed for me. I had trouble breathing for an hour or two. They were going to wait another 15 minutes, and if I didn't start breathing, they were going to cut a hole in my throat so I could. But about 10 minutes later, I started to wake up and breathe again.

The police officers told me my blood alcohol level was .59, which can cause death. I had to go to counseling for six months after this incident. My whole family was involved.

Now I am healthy and alcohol-free because I was lucky.

I hope this story will help teen-agers stop drinking. Believe me, the fascination with alcohol is not worth your life.

Some of you probably never heard of alcohol being a killer, because I didn't before this happened to me. But now it's time to stop before it's too late.

I will never drink again and I really don't want to. It used to be hard not being able to drink around my friends when they were. But I got through it, and so can you.

Please, just take a moment to stop and think that this could happen to you. I always thought that nothing would happen to me. But I was wrong and so are you.

Alcohol and the Adolescent Brain

Scott Swartzwelder

Most people know that drinking can cause you to lose your inhibitions, but what really happens when alcohol reaches your brain? Scientists such as Scott Swartzwelder have been studying this question. He writes here that the brains of teens are especially vulnerable to alcohol because their brains are still growing and developing. Alcohol may retard their mental growth. Swartzwelder is a professor of psychology and psychiatry at Duke University Medical Center. He is a coauthor of *Buzzed: The Straight Facts About the Most Used and Abused Drugs; from Alcohol to Ecstasy.*

Not long ago, most people believed that the brain was virtually finished developing soon after birth, and that there was little change until aging occurred. However, the newest research shows that the brain continues to develop throughout childhood and adolescence until approximately age 20.

The developing brain is different from the adult brain in its ability to change in response to experience. For example, the young brain appears to be "built to learn." This uniqueness of the adolescent brain creates great opportunities.

Reprinted from Scott Swartzwelder, "Brain 101," *Driven*, Fall 1998. Reprinted with permission from the author.

However, there's a darker side. For 15 years, my laboratory group at the Duke University and Durham Veterans Administration Medical Centers has been examining the effects of alcohol on the brain. Our published research shows that the brain responds to alcohol differently during adolescence than during adulthood. In some ways alcohol is more powerful, while in other ways it's less powerful. These differences spell bad news when it comes to teen drinking and driving.

Alcohol and Pregnancy

Drinking alcohol during pregnancy can cause physical and mental birth defects. Each year, more than 50,000 babies are born with some degree of alcohol-related damage. Although many women are aware that heavy drinking during pregnancy can cause birth defects, many do not realize that moderate—or even light—drinking also may harm the fetus. . . .

When a pregnant woman drinks, alcohol passes swiftly through the placenta to her fetus. In the unborn baby's immature body, alcohol is broken down much more slowly than in an adult's body. As a result, the alcohol level of the fetus's blood can be even higher and can remain elevated longer than in the mother's blood. This sometimes causes the baby to suffer life-long damage.

March of Dimes, "Drinking Alcohol During Pregnancy," 1998.

In experiments studying brain circuits in rats, we compared the effects of alcohol on the function of a brain chemical that is critical for mental function. Alcohol impaired the sensitivity of the brain to this chemical much more in adolescents than in adults. In the adolescent brain, this activity was impaired by the equivalent of about one drink. When it comes to learning, adolescent animals were impaired by much lower doses of alcohol than adults.

Our studies on people also produced striking results. Because of the 21 minimum drinking age law, we studied people ages 21–29. Alcohol impaired learning much more in 21–24-year-olds than in those just a few years older at 25–29. During young adulthood, alcohol is a very potent drug, and it interferes with memory formation. The effects might be even more striking in teens.

But the more we learned, the more interesting the findings became. Again, using animal models, we found that high doses of alcohol were much less sedative in adolescents than in adults. Adolescents were less likely to be put to sleep by alcohol; when they did go to sleep, they slept for much less time. Thus, alcohol may make adolescents less sleepy than adults.

But this does not mean that it's safer for teens to drink and drive than for adults. The opposite probably is true. The adolescent may be able to drink more than an adult before becoming sleepy enough to stop, but meanwhile she is further impairing mental functions important for safe driving. Just because you can get behind the wheel doesn't mean you should. The brain functions that control sleepiness aren't the same ones that control judgement and decision making. A teen may stay awake enough to drive after drinking, but still make very bad decisions about how to drive or whether to drive in the first place.

> Research shows that the brain responds to alcohol differently during adolescence than during adulthood.

Our teens need to know what the scientific research clearly suggests: that adolescents have exactly the wrong pattern of sensitivities to alcohol. It's not enough to tell young people "don't drink because we say so," and they won't accept scare tactics that aren't based on established facts. But a conversation about how unique their brains are could be lifesaving—for themselves and everyone else on our roads.

Alcohol Myths

Mothers Against Drunk Driving (MADD)

Alcohol gives you energy. A cold shower or cup of coffee will sober someone up. These are two of many false beliefs some people have about alcohol. Mothers Against Drunk Driving (MADD) attempts to dispel these and other myths about alcohol and its effects.

It's time to blast some of the most wacked-out lies about alcohol. You've probably heard them all. So, why waste our time trying to debunk a bunch of harmless myths? Because they can be pretty fierce.

You may want to say no to your friends, but it's tough. And all these myths are just out there. You have heard all kinds of stuff, but this is the real story. And the next time some loser tries these lines on you, you'll know your stuff.

Myth *Alcohol gives you energy.* Nope. It's a depressant. It slows down your ability to think, speak, move and all that other silly stuff you like to do.

Myth *Switching between beer, wine and liquor will make you more drunk than sticking to one type of alcohol.* Whatever! Your blood alcohol content (BAC—the percent of alcohol in your blood) is what determines how drunk you are. Not the flavors you selected. Alcohol is alcohol.

Myth *You'll get drunk a lot quicker with hard liquor than with*

Reprinted from "Some Myths About Alcohol," MADD (www.madd.org). Reprinted with permission from *Driven* magazine.

a beer or wine cooler. Did we mention that alcohol is alcohol?

Myth *Everybody reacts the same to alcohol.* Not hardly. There are dozens of factors that affect reactions to alcohol—body weight, time of day, how you feel mentally, body chemistry, your expectations, and the list goes on and on.

Tips for Teens About Alcohol

1. Know the law. Alcohol is illegal to buy or possess if you are under 21.

2. Get the facts right. One 12-ounce beer has as much alcohol as a 1.5-ounce shot of whiskey or a 5-ounce glass of wine.

3. Stay informed. Wine coolers look like juice sparklers but they have just as much alcohol as a 12-ounce beer. One glass of clear malt can give a teenager a .02 on a breathalyzer test. In some states that amount is enough for anyone under the age of 21 to lose his/her driver's license and be subject to a fine.

4. Be aware of the risks. Drinking increases the risk of injury. Car crashes, falls, burns, drowning, and suicide are all linked to alcohol and other drug use.

5. Keep your edge. Alcohol can ruin your looks, give you bad breath, and make you gain weight.

6. Play it safe. Drinking can lead to intoxication and even death.

7. Do the smart thing. Drinking puts your health, education, family ties, and social life at risk.

8. Be a real friend. If you know someone with a drinking problem, be part of the solution. Urge your friend to get help.

9. Remain alert. Stay clear on claims that alcohol means glamour and adventure. Stay clear on what's real and what's illusion.

10. Sweep away the myths. Having a designated driver is no excuse to drink. Drinking only at home, or sticking only to beer does not make drinking any "safer."

"Tips for Teens About Alcohol," Center for Substance Abuse Prevention.

Myth *A cold show or a cup of coffee will sober someone up.* Not on your life. Nothing sobers you up but time. You may be clean and awake, but you're still drunk.

Myth *It's just beer. It can't permanently damage you.* Large amounts of alcohol can do major damage to your digestive system. You can hurt your heart, liver, stomach, and several other critical organs as well as losing years from your life.

Myth *It's none of my business if a friend is drinking too much.* If you are a real friend, it is your business. You can't make someone change but you can be honest. Maybe they'll listen. You might even talk them into getting help.

Myth *The worst thing that can happen is a raging hangover.* Sorry. If you drink enough alcohol, fast enough, you can get an amount in your body that can kill you in only a few hours.

Myth *Drugs are a bigger problem than alcohol.* Alcohol and tobacco kill more than 50 times the number of people killed by cocaine, heroin, and every other illegal drug combined. Ten million Americans are addicted to alcohol. It is a drug.

Myth *Alcohol makes you more sexy.* The more you drink, the less you think. Alcohol may loosen you up and make someone more interested in sex, but it interferes with the body's ability to perform. And then there's pregnancy, AIDS, sexual assault, car crashes and worse, to worry about. Not sexy at all.

Myth *People who drink too much only hurt themselves.* Every person who drinks has a mother, grandfather, sister, aunt, best friend, boyfriend or girlfriend who worries about them. Each of the 12 million problem drinkers in this country affects four other people.

Alcohol and Sex

Jim Parker

Many adults—and teens—drink as a way to lower their inhibitions in an attempt to make it all right to engage in sex. However, a writer for a drug abuse education foundation argues that alcohol's ability to reduce inhibitions and impair judgment can result in unsafe sex, unwanted pregnancies, and sexually transmitted diseases. And contrary to what beer commercials may tell you, alcohol abuse can lead to impotence and other sexual problems.

Let's look at what [alcohol] does in the mind, and consider why people drink.

The two issues are pretty closely linked. Because the main reasons people give when they're asked why they drink involve the psychological payoffs they say they get from booze: to relax and feel less self-conscious, to fit in or be sociable or express themselves better.

But if you look deeper, you often see something else underneath, and find such unacknowledged reasons as depression, loneliness, low self-esteem, and other problems.

And that's worth thinking about, because something that researchers have consistently noted over the years is that people who drink to escape problems or pump up their self-confidence

Excerpted from Jim Parker, "Booze: The Basics and Beyond," an online article found at www.doitnow.org/pages/130.html. Reprinted with permission from the Do It Now Foundation.

are more likely to become problem drinkers. And problem drinking creates even bigger problems.

Drinking and Sex

Then there's sex. It may just be the biggest unacknowledged reason for drinking of all. As American humorist Ogden Nash pointed out a long time ago ("Candy is dandy, but liquor is quicker"), alcohol can work wonders in turning a simple attraction into a serious affair.

The problem is that it can also turn a night out into a nightmare.

Just ask the tens of thousands of young people who turned into young parents last year, when normal sex drives got even more inflamed with alcohol.

> Drinking and unsafe sex go together like, well, unsafe sex and AIDS.

And if you don't believe them, ask the thousands of kids who get caught up every year in allegations of date rape: He says she was asking for it. She says she was only asking him to stop.

Alcohol's ability to deflate inhibitions as it inflates desire hasn't been lost on advertisers, either—at least not those willing to capitalize on human weakness and insecurities, which includes most of them.

Beer Advertisements

That's why beer commercials have traditionally been among the most sexually-oriented ads on TV.

Advertisers pull out all the stops—in the form of giggles and wiggles at bars and on beaches—to sell lonely people on a single idea: Drink our beer and you might get lucky. *These guys did.*

The problem is that drinkers usually don't get lucky—and even when they do, they *don't.*

Because studies show that drinking and unsafe sex go together like, well, unsafe sex and AIDS. Drinkers just don't see what all the fuss is about and, besides, they're invulnerable anyway, right?

A final item to consider in reviewing the relationship between sex and alcohol is something [playwright William] Shakespeare noted hundreds of years ago, when he pointed out that alcohol "provokes the desire but it takes away the performance."

Scientific studies and clinical reports bear out the Bard's conclusion, as do problem drinkers themselves, who often report sexual problems, ranging from impotence and frigidity to outright *deterioration* of the sexual organs.

Need any other motivation to not get blasted on a regular basis?

Chapter 2

Alcoholism and Problem Drinking

What Is Alcoholism?

Hayley R. Mitchell

Although most people who drink do so in moderation and do not become addicted to alcohol, some wind up abusing alcohol and suffering severe consequences. Hayley R. Mitchell, an author and writing teacher, briefly explains the symptoms and stages of alcohol dependence or alcoholism. She also describes the steps alcoholics can take to treat their condition. An important part of recovery from alcoholism for many is participating in Alcoholics Anonymous (AA) and similar self-help programs, including some designed for teens.

A lcoholism, also known as alcohol dependence syndrome, is a disease characterized by cravings, loss of control, physical dependence, and a need for more and more alcohol. Alcoholics crave alcohol in that they have a strong need, or compulsion, to drink. And, commonly, alcoholics share an inability to stop drinking. In other words, although alcoholics may be aware of the disruptive effects alcohol is having on their lives, their physical and emotional dependence on alcohol is so strong that they cannot give it up.

While some people who abuse alcohol may have an emotional dependence on the drug, alcoholics also have a physical de-

Excerpted from Hayley R. Mitchell, *Teen Alcoholism*, San Diego: Lucent Books, 1998.

pendence on alcohol. Physical dependence is characterized by the occurrence of withdrawal symptoms, such as nausea, sweating, shakiness, and anxiety, if alcohol use is suspended. Alcoholics relieve these symptoms by resuming drinking or by taking other sedative drugs.

Developing a tolerance to alcohol is also a sign of alcoholism. Building a tolerance to alcohol simply means that heavy drinkers eventually need more and more alcohol to feel its intoxicating effects. Roger E. Vogler, in his book *Teenagers & Alcohol: When Saying No Isn't Enough,* defines tolerance well. "If you drink every day," he says, "developing some long-term tolerance is inevitable. After a period of time, because two drinks no longer provide the high they once did, you may now have to consume three drinks to get the same effect that two drinks used to produce. After a while when three doesn't seem to do it, you move up to four drinks."

Phases of Alcoholism

An increase in tolerance to alcohol usually develops in what [authors Jean] Kinney and [Gwen] Leaton describe as the "pre-alcoholic" phase. Typically, during this phase, a person seeks out alcohol in social situations. Someone who is likely to become an alcoholic will begin to feel some kind of psychological relief from drinking in a social atmosphere. Psychological dependence may develop when this person begins to need to drink in order to do something, such as face a difficult task, loosen up sexually, have a good time, or unwind at the end of the day.

> Developing a tolerance to alcohol is also a sign of alcoholism.

Soon the drinker may exhibit other warning signs of alcoholism. For instance, he or she may experience blackouts, or memory lapses, when drinking. The drinker may begin to drink alone before going out to parties, to gulp drinks, and to feel some guilt about his or her drinking.

The next phase, or "crucial phase," is one in which drinkers tend to lose control of their drinking. Drinkers in this phase are "alternatively resentful, remorseful, and aggressive," Kinney and Leaton note. "Life has become alcohol centered. Family life and friendships deteriorate. The first alcohol-related hospitalization is likely." At this stage, the alcoholic has developed a physical dependence on alcohol. His or her body needs the neurochemical reaction produced by alcohol to function.

The final phase in the process of alcoholism is the "chronic phase," in which drinking begins earlier in the day and drunkenness is usually a daily state. In this phase the alcoholic may turn to drinking in places outside his or her peer group, such as bars outside the neighborhood. The alcoholic may notice a loss of tolerance to alcohol in this phase, and may develop tremors (shaking). Ultimately, Kinney and Leaton say alcoholics may be so determined to drink that they will drink anything containing alcohol, including rubbing alcohol. . . .

> The final phase in the process of alcoholism is the "chronic" phase in which . . . drunkenness is usually a daily state.

Treatment of Alcoholism

Alcoholism . . . is treatable, and the sooner a person is able to acknowledge a need for help, the better are his or her chances for recovery. The types of programs suitable for alcoholics vary. The severity of an individual's drinking problem and available community resources, for example, are factors to be considered when choosing rehabilitation programs.

Some alcoholics seek treatment in hospital or residential-care settings. In these cases, they move into the facilities until they can get their drinking under control. Other alcoholics may select treatment on an outpatient basis: This choice is most appropriate for patients who do not want to interrupt their daily work or living arrangements. In both options, treatment may include detoxification, which is the process of slowly and safely getting alcohol out of the patient's system; prescribed medications, which help prevent patients from returning to drinking after they have stopped; and individual or group counseling.

Medications and Counseling

When alcoholics first seek treatment after periods of heavy, continuous drinking, there is a strong likelihood that they will suffer withdrawal symptoms, including seizures and hallucinations. These symptoms generally last from five to eight days, and they can be treated with medication in a hospital or clinic.

In addition to receiving drugs for withdrawal management, patients may later be prescribed medications, such as anticraving agents, that decrease the desire for alcohol consumption. Other medications can be taken that provoke negative physical reactions, such as vomiting, when alcohol is ingested, reinforcing a patient's willingness not to drink. Finally, drugs are also available that reverse the intoxicating effects of alcohol. Should an alcoholic who is on these drugs decide to drink, he or she would be unable to get drunk.

> Alcoholism . . . is treatable, and the sooner a person is able to acknowledge a need for help, the better are his or her chances for recovery.

Although alcoholism is treatable, there is no guarantee that an alcoholic will stop drinking. After they have regained health through medical treatment, alcoholics must make an effort every day to remain sober. The prevailing opinion is that alcoholics cannot just cut down on their drinking. They must avoid all alcoholic beverages if they are to achieve complete, long-term sobriety. On the road to sobriety, relapses, brief or extended periods of drinking, are very common.

To help prevent relapses, health professionals recommend alcoholics join "aftercare" counseling programs as part of their treatment. There are a number of counseling groups available to alcoholics that help alcoholics commit to a lifetime of sobriety. These groups include confidential self-help organizations that offer assistance to anyone who has a drinking problem and wants to deal with it.

In counseling, alcoholics are taught how to identify feelings and situations in their lives that may lead them to drink. They are encouraged to find new, positive ways of dealing with these situations that do not include drinking alcohol. There is generally no fee for the services of these counseling organizations. In addition, meetings are held in most communities, and friends and family members are often encouraged to attend.

Alcoholics Anonymous

One of the most widely adapted aftercare programs is Alcoholics Anonymous (AA). AA is a so-called twelve-step, mutual help program that stresses spiritual growth. As a first step, all members of AA are asked to admit that they are alcoholics who cannot manage their own lives. They recognize that "no human power could have relieved" their alcoholism. In this light, many of the twelve steps dictate that members place their faith in God in order to reach full recovery. Step three, for example, involves making "a decision to turn our will and our lives over to the care of God as we understand him."

Studies show that belief in the twelve-step philosophy of AA, not necessarily the number of meetings attended, is important to the recovery process. Another important aspect of AA is sponsorship. In AA, longtime members "sponsor" newer members to help them reach sobriety. Studies show that such sponsorship has a strong impact on sobriety. For example, 91 percent of AA sponsors report complete or stable remission of alcoholism.

Sobriety High

Although teen alcoholism treatment programs include the same treatment options as adult programs, many teens prefer these programs because they can recover from their addictions with others their age. Like adult programs, teen treatment centers encourage the development of peer resistance, social skills, and relapse-prevention techniques.

There are numerous traditional, teen-oriented treatment centers, as well as some programs in less traditional settings, throughout the United States. One special program, for example, is Sobriety High, in Edina, Minnesota, where, Roberta Myers writes, "staying off drugs and alcohol is not only cool but a graduation requirement." Up to forty-three students can attend Sobriety High, instead of their regular high schools, at one time. They must be diagnosed as chemically dependent, and they must have completed drug- or alcohol-addiction programs before they can be admitted. In addition, students must sign a contract, pledging to remain sober.

> There are a number of counseling groups available to alcoholics that help alcoholics commit to a lifetime of sobriety.

Unlike traditional high schools, Sobriety High students graduate in six, not four, years. Sobriety High also assigns no homework. Instead, students spend their afterschool time working through their addictions. They meet with school counselors, for example, and many also attend AA meetings or other counseling groups. Despite the no-homework policy, students who graduate from Sobriety High receive the same level of education as other public schools in Minnesota. The state board of education sets curriculum, and grades, Myers writes, are based on "attendance, participation, in-class assignments, and tests."

Sobriety High founder Ralph Neiditch believes that the school is a haven for alcohol- and drug-addicted teens. The "worst place for kids with drug problems," he says, "is high school, where drinking and getting high are so common." At Sobriety High, these teens not only escape the drug environments of their schools and neighborhoods, they also learn respect for themselves and others. One sixteen-year-old, Jay, says, "They really care about you here. They listen to your problems and don't just say 'We'll get over it.'"

Sobriety High not only teaches respect, but also forces teens to take a serious look at the effects of their addictions. Sixteen-year-old student Sarah Smith, who began drinking heavily at age eleven, says that Sobriety High helped her to "confront the shame she felt about using, about being used, and about how much she hurt her mom." She says, "If I weren't sober I could be pregnant, I could be kicked out of my house—who knows where I'd be?" In 1995 Sarah was beginning to look forward to graduating and attending college. She says that she'll accept her diploma with pride. "That diploma stands for a lot," she says. "It says I'm sober," and, she adds, "I've accomplished something. Something a hell of a lot harder than most people ever will."

Alcohol Abuse Among Teens: A Growing National Problem

Stephen Williams

Alcoholism is as serious a problem among teenagers as it is for adults. The following article by Stephen Williams examines the problem of teen alcohol abuse. Part of the problem, he believes, is a shortage of alcoholism treatment and prevention programs designed for teens. Several teens tell how they became addicted to alcohol, and what they did to recover control over their lives.

[Editor's note: Names of teens discussed in this article have been changed.]

Sarah had a problem from the moment she took her first drink, when she was 12. "Right from the beginning, I drank to blackout," says the 18-year-old, who is now a freshman at Haverford College outside Philadelphia. She says friends and people at school knew that she drank, but because she still passed her tests and did well in sports, no one at school or at home believed she really had a problem.

Until one day in 10th grade, when Sarah showed up raving

drunk for a school softball game. The truth was finally out. School officials gave her two choices: Go to rehab or be expelled. "They wanted to punish me, not help," says Sarah, whose drinking got so bad that she eventually tried to commit suicide by swallowing 42 prescription pills. "I used the rehab more for making new connections than for getting sober." Maybe if Sarah had been able to talk to a trained counselor at her school, or a peer group for similarly troubled teens, things would have been different. But those choices simply weren't available to her.

As it turns out, those choices aren't available in most of America. "The denial in society is rampant," says Ann D. Miller, an intervention specialist at Canby High School, outside Portland, Ore. "It's as if we're saying, 'If we don't offer counselors for teenage alcoholics, then we don't have a problem.' Many schools have to charge students to play football," she adds. "Do you think they're going to find money to hire an alcohol counselor?"

A National Problem

And yet, national statistics point to an alarming need for counselors, peer groups and prevention programs to address the issue of underage drinking in this country. An estimated one in five teens runs a high risk of becoming an alcoholic, and those who start drinking before age 15 are four times more likely to have a problem later in life than those who wait until they're 21. A survey found that 4.4 million American teens indulge in monthly drinking binges. *The New York Times* reported that 16 percent of teens have blacked out as a result of drinking alcohol, and, according to a 1999 federal survey, one in three high school seniors has tossed back five or more drinks at least once in the last two weeks. "There's a real sense of urgency about helping these young drinkers," says Ariel White-Kovach, executive director of youth services for Minnesota's Hazelden Foundation. "Options for youths are few and far between."

That certainly was the case for 17-year-old Audra Lucas. "I've always felt like the odd person out," she says. Growing up in Chowchilla, Calif., she went to her first AA meeting at age 13. "But it was just a bunch of old people in this church basement and I couldn't relate," says Audra, who at five feet five inches and 115 pounds could still put away 14 beers before blacking out. In the past five years, Audra has never been able to stay sober for more than a few months at a time.

> National statistics point to an alarming need for counselors, peer groups and prevention programs to address the issue of underage drinking in this country.

Not that she hasn't tried—time and time again. During her freshman year, she got so bombed on 151-proof rum one night that she wound up in the emergency room, where doctors pumped her stomach. Audra looked into outpatient counseling, but couldn't afford it herself—and she was too ashamed to talk to her family. "There wasn't anyone to help me at school," she says. "There wasn't anyone anywhere. In a way, that was a relief—it meant I could go back to drinking."

Finally, after another blackout, Audra talked to her mom, who helped her find a group called Kids in Sobriety (KIS). Based in Ventura and founded by addiction treatment specialist Debbie Hughes, KIS is one of the few programs in the country geared specifically to teens. Designed to be affordable, it offers peer group counseling, long-term support and group visits to AA meetings. Parents are required to attend counseling, which is key to helping their kids stay sober. "Parents are usually in denial about what their kids are doing," says Hughes. "We want the kid to be safe to say, 'I really feel like getting loaded, can you help me not do that?' Parents have to learn to take their children's problem seriously."

Permissive Parents

In fact, parents often contribute to the problem. Studies show that kids whose parents forbid them to drink until they're 21 are less likely to become drunks. "But around here," says Kasey Folse, a 17-year-old junior at Pineville High School in Pineville, La., "parents will buy alcohol for the kids, thinking, 'As long as they're drinking at home with us, they're safe.' Then the kids think it's OK to drink anywhere. That's wrong. I mean, as parents, would you let your kids have sex at home? They're both serious problems." Adds Ann Miller, "This is happening all over. We have parents who seem unable to say, 'You can't drink.' We have adults who rent motel rooms for their kids, buy them booze and then act surprised when they get in trouble. I say, 'Hellooooo? Is anybody home?'"

A member of the Louisiana Alliance to Prevent Underage Drinking, Kasey works to enact laws that make it harder for teens to buy alcohol, such as registration tags for beer kegs. But there's still plenty of drinking at her school. "Kids don't really have anywhere to turn at my school," says Kasey. "It would definitely help if we had someone to go one-on-one with students to deal with alcohol and drug problems. It would be a full-time job."

Things weren't all that different at Andrew Araiza's Mary Carroll High School in Corpus Christi, Texas. "I drank too much in my freshman year," says Andrew, 18, who's now at the University of Texas. "My grades went down, I didn't care about anything. I put my family through such pain." Andrew says underage drinking was so accepted in Corpus Christi that many adults basically seemed happy as long as he wasn't doing drugs. "They don't consider all the problems associated with alcohol, like poisoning, rape and suicide," says Andrew, who finally quit on his own after his dad threatened to send him to military camp. "They just see drinking as a normal thing."

The Need for Treatment and Education

Now, as executive vice president of Texans Standing Tall, a coalition of youths and adults against underage drinking, Andrew has successfully lobbied to remove liquor ads from the state's hunting license handbook, and helped lower the legal blood alcohol limit from .1 to .08. "I want to keep others from going through what I went through," he says. "Having peer group talks, where a teen with a problem describes what happened to him—that would get the message across."

> In the past five years, Audra has never been able to stay sober for more than a few months at a time.

Thanks to Ann Miller, that message is coming through loud and clear at Oregon's Canby High. She educates teens about drinking, counsels those with problems and encourages them to attend a local youth-oriented AA meeting. The result is a heightened awareness in the school of the drawbacks of alcohol use, and a population of teens who aren't afraid to ask for help. "It's a myth that teens won't get better over the long haul," says Miller, who sees five or six new kids each week. "But they've got to have good treatment available and good support from the adults around them."

Unfortunately for Sarah, that just wasn't an option. Desperate to get sober, and realizing she could rely only on herself, Sarah found a job, started saving money for rehab—and continued drinking just enough to keep the withdrawal shakes away. Last March 1999, she spent 28 days in a Pittsburgh rehab, and now, thanks to regular AA meetings, she has been sober 10 months. "I'm lucky," says Sarah, "because a lot of kids out there are falling through the cracks."

An Alcoholic at Twelve

Shandra O'Connell, as told to Lambeth Hochwald

Shandra O'Connell, a high school student and recovering alcoholic, tells her personal story of how she started drinking when she was eleven years old and how alcohol came to dominate her life. Alcohol at first made her feel comfortable with herself and her circle of friends, but it also led to failing grades at school and an unwanted pregnancy. She eventually sought treatment for alcoholism at a hospital and halfway house, and now attends a special high school for recovering drug and alcohol addicts.

When my mom and I moved from Pennsylvania to Minnesota, things got tough. I started middle school and I didn't know anyone. We were all put in this class called "home base" for the first three days of school, where I got to know a girl who introduced me to her friends—a bad crowd, but I didn't realize it at the time. I immediately fell in with that group and at 11 years old I started drinking alcohol with them.

In the beginning, we'd drink every now and then, or we'd get wine coolers for the school dance. Then we started drinking every weekend—hard liquor, usually mixed with juice so it would taste good. Then I began skipping school a few days a week to get drunk with my friends instead. Toward the end of

Reprinted from Shandra O'Connell, interviewed by Lambeth Hochwald, "I Was an Alcoholic at 12 Years Old," *Teen*, December 1999. Reprinted with permission from Lambeth Hochwald.

sixth grade, getting loaded became an everyday thing for me.

Drinking made me more comfortable with who I was; I didn't care what people thought of me. I could be the loud person everyone liked and my friends told me I was the funniest person when I was wasted. And it was easy to get our hands on alcohol. Most of the time, older friends would get it for us. I even had a boyfriend once whose parents would buy it for us, no problem.

To keep my habit hidden from my mother, I stayed at friends' houses or I'd drink during school; in the bathroom or parking lot. If I came home a little buzzed, I'd wear perfume or eat something to get the smell of alcohol off my body. I don't know if she had a clue or if she was in denial, but if she suspected something, she didn't say anything.

My life was starting to fall apart, but I was too "gone" to see it. My friends and I started experimenting with hard drugs—it just seemed natural. It got so bad that I was never able to think straight—and the Ds and Fs I started getting in class proved that. I hardly even went to school, but I didn't care. And I can't even count the number of times I blacked out at parties or wherever. I remember waking up drunk lots of times, and I had no clue what I did the night before; someone would have to tell me.

Liquor made me really promiscuous, and guys took advantage of that. I got pregnant when I was 12 years old, and to this day, I honestly don't know who the father is, which is really sad. I kept the pregnancy a secret from my mom at first. But when I was five months pregnant, and still drinking, my best friend's mom told my mother. She was really shocked. Right then, I just quit everything, including smoking cigarettes. I didn't want to harm the baby. My mom told me I should give the baby up for adoption, which I did. I'm not mad about it; I couldn't make that decision for myself at 13 when I had the baby.

> Drinking made me more comfortable with who I was; I didn't care what people thought of me.

How a Teenager Can Tell If Drinking Is a Problem

Every "Yes" answer is a warning sign to stop and consider where you are going and what might happen. More than four "Yes" answers means you should seek help.

	YES	NO
1. Do you lose time from school because of drinking?	___	___
2. Do you drink to lose shyness and build up self-confidence?	___	___
3. Is drinking affecting your reputation?	___	___
4. Do you drink to escape from study or home worries?	___	___
5. Does it bother you if somebody says maybe you drink too much?	___	___
6. Do you have to take a drink to go out on a date?	___	___
7. Do you ever get into money trouble over buying liquor?	___	___
8. Have you lost friends since you've started drinking?	___	___
9. Do you hang out now with a crowd where stuff is easy to get?	___	___
10. Do your friends drink less than you do?	___	___
11. Do you drink until the bottle is empty?	___	___
12. Have you ever had a loss of memory from drinking?	___	___
13. Has drunk driving ever put you into the hospital or jail?	___	___
14. Do you get annoyed with classes or lectures on drinking?	___	___
15. Do you think you have a problem with liquor?	___	___

Ralph Jones, *Straight Talk: Answers to Questions Young People Ask About Alcohol*, 1988.

When I was pregnant, I went to a teen pregnancy school, but after I had the baby, I went back to regular middle school—right back to the same crowd and my old ways. This time I ran away a lot. I craved freedom, and I wanted to be with my friends. Sometimes I wouldn't come home for a night, and sometimes I was away for days. Once, my friend and I stole her mom's car for two days. We called another friend and found our mothers waiting for us at her house. My mom would do whatever she could to find me when I ran away. One time she came to pick me up at a friend's house and she didn't even recognize me because I was covered in blood from cutting myself up when I was out-of-my-mind-drunk.

> My life was starting to fall apart, but I was too "gone" to see it.

The last time I ran away, I was gone for two days and I was taking drugs and drinking the entire time. I was really strung out—and I suddenly realized it. The only way to explain it is that when you're on drugs and haven't slept, you analyze everything. I knew I had to stop. I wanted to be sober, so I looked for help.

I came home and the counselor I'd been seeing sent me to a hospital. I spent a week in a locked unit. I was searched, and they went through all my stuff. It was hell, and it was horrible not having any alcohol or drugs; it was like my security was taken away. After those seven days, they recommended a three-month halfway house to continue treatment. I graduated from the halfway house in May 1998 and I've been sober ever since—for 22 months.

A girl at the halfway house had told me about Sobriety High and how cool it was. It's a high school for students going through some kind of recovery, either from drugs or alcohol. My mom and I got an application. I had to write an essay on why I wanted to go there, and I was accepted. Sobriety High is like a second family. We played trust games at first, so we could get to know each other, but now we have normal classes and then one hour of group therapy every day. About three times a week, after school, I go to meetings for recovering alcoholics. I'm in the eleventh grade now and I've been on the honor roll the entire time I've been here.

These days, most of my friends are totally different from the ones I knew when I was drinking. They're real friends as opposed to the people in my past, who would lie to me or screw me over. I've heard about one or two who have gotten sober, but the majority haven't.

I blame this mess on myself—for not having any self-respect. I also had incredibly low self-esteem. I don't blame my mom at all. It's just been me and my mom for almost 12 years, although now she's remarried. For a while, she was the only one taking care of me. She's the one who made me stick to soccer. (I'd play while drunk a lot of the time, and I don't even know how I kept my balance or how my coach never suspected a thing, but soccer was the one place I could get away and be myself.) My mom tells me she's proud of me all the time. Even little things make her proud. We were shopping the other day and I told her there were so many things I want to do with my life and she started crying.

> These days, most of my friends are totally different from the ones I knew when I was drinking.

The amazing thing is that I hadn't had a real home or family life since I was 11 or 12 because I was always on the run, or I'd just come home to take a shower or change my clothes. I'm kinda making up for lost time now. For the past year-and-a-half I've been focusing on clothes and boys—normal girl things!

Since I quit drinking, I feel healthier, I eat right and I'm sleeping better. I'm taking showers and brushing my teeth. I don't have dark circles under my eyes. I think I look better. I even want to get into modeling. I just take it day by day. Being sober is my life; it's my daily routine.

Problem Drinking

Mark Worden

Mark Worden, a writer for a drug abuse education organization, begins by telling the story of Tony, a teenage alcoholic. Worden goes on to state that problem drinking can take many forms, not all of which are cases of full-blown alcoholism. He provides real examples of people who are not alcoholics, but are instead "careless drinkers" whose lives have been harmed by alcohol. Young people are especially prone to careless drinking, he warns.

Tony never understood why his father drank so much until he "borrowed" a bottle from his dad's liquor cabinet. He drank the whole thing with two guys he hung with after school.

The liquor burned Tony's throat at first, but the sting soon changed to a fuzzy warmth that crept over his body like a blanket. His inhibitions melted, he laughed, and he felt happy for a while.

When he sobered up, the happiness left him, replaced by a vague guilt. But there was also a memory: euphoria, freedom, fun. A few hours of not caring, not worrying. That made him look forward to his next chance to drink, to be free again.

And that's exactly what he did. He began to "borrow" from his father's liquor stash regularly. His dad was so out of it most of the time that he didn't notice. Tony learned to sneak money

Reprinted from Mark Worden, "Problem Drinking & Alcoholism: Words to the Wise," an online article found at www.doitnow.org/pages/801.html. Reprinted with permission from the Do It Now Foundation.

out of his mother's purse and shoplift "40's"—40-ounce bottles of malt liquor—from the store when he didn't have money.

At first, Tony's friends joined in. But after a while, they realized there was something wrong with the way Tony drank. He'd beg, lie, and steal for a drink. He was hooked; he was a teenage alcoholic.

Tony is just one kind of problem drinker. There are lots of others. Substance abuse education programs teach students to be alert to the symptoms of alcoholism, including:

- Emotional and/or physical dependence on alcohol
- Sneaking drinks, hiding bottles, drinking alone
- Loss of control over drinking
- Drinking in the morning to control shakes
- Physical symptoms if drinking stops

Still, there are other signs of a drinking problem. And they often go unrecognized.

One in Twenty

Something else that often goes unrecognized is the extent of the problem.

Think of it this way: If you have twenty friends, odds are that one of them will become alcoholic, physically addicted to alcohol.

Alcohol addiction is usually slow to develop, often taking 5-10 years of heavy drinking before a person is physically hooked. This contrasts sharply with many other drugs, which can cause addiction in a matter of weeks.

And since physical addiction develops so slowly, a person can have problems for years before anyone points a finger and says, "Hey, maybe you should cut down on your drinking."

That's the kicker. We usually don't consider a person to have a drinking problem until he or she has developed into a full-blown alcoholic, until they're physically hooked, until their life is a total mess.

What we don't seem to realize is that drinking problems take a lot of forms and usually develop long before we identify someone as an alcoholic.

And many people who never become alcoholics experience all kinds of life problems that stem directly from drinking too much.

> Drinking problems take a lot of forms and usually develop long before we identify someone as an alcoholic.

And people whose lives they touch—family, friends, and co-workers—often get hit by the fallout.

In other words, although only one in twenty may have an alcohol problem, lots of people are affected by people who drink irresponsibly.

And there are almost an infinite number of ways to do that.

The following examples are real, with the names changed to protect anonymity.

War Stories

• Diane and Steve, both seniors in high school, had been dating for several months. One night they got drunk and had unprotected sex.

The result? Diane got pregnant and, even though they weren't sure they belonged together, they got married. The marriage lasted two years. Now she's raising their son alone, working at a low-paying job, and is far from happy.

• Paul didn't drink very often, but when he did, he got belligerent. He mouthed off, insulted friends, and was generally surly. He called it "livin' large."

One night he made the mistake of directing a graphic sexual come-on to a woman in a bar, and tried to fondle her. She smashed him in the face, then called the police. The judge dismissed the charges against Paul, but the dentist charged $600 to fix the teeth that had been broken when the woman hit him.

• Suzanne wasn't very popular, so when she was invited to a

party by a co-worker at her office, she was excited. At the party, though, she felt nervous and out of place. She threw down several margaritas back to back, hoping that would loosen her up.

It did. She started telling dirty jokes and laughing hysterically. Then she got sick. She threw up all over herself, several friends, and the furniture. Then she passed out and had to be carried home.

> Most young people who drink do it carelessly.

On Monday, half the office had heard about it. They don't call her Suzanne any more. Now it's "Margarita."

• Danny's parents let him use the car on the condition he never drink and drive. One night, after drinking a six-pack of beer, he was driving home when he saw an explosion of flashing blue lights behind him.

Danny tried to outrun the police, but lost control of the car on a curve and crashed into a telephone pole. He not only totaled his parent's car, but broke both his legs.

Careless Drinkers

Diane, Paul, Suzanne, and Danny aren't alcoholics, yet they all suffered problems caused by irresponsible drinking. We'll call them careless drinkers.

Careless drinkers are people who occasionally drink too much and are sometimes embarrassed or troubled by things that happen when they drink.

Their problems often result from the situations and context they drink in, not because they have deep emotional problems, or because they're alcoholics. They don't experience a lot of problems because of alcohol, and their lives aren't falling apart, but their problems are real.

Young people, especially, tend to be careless drinkers. In fact, most young people who drink do it carelessly. They may not drink daily, but when they do drink, they often do it with the sole purpose of getting drunk. They often drink fast and they drink a lot.

They also run into other problems. Women and girls report unwanted sexual experiences after drinking too much. Speeding cars end up in ditches. Every weekend, thousands of drinkers wake up with throbbing headaches and agonizing memories about what they did the night before—when they can remember it.

You don't have to be like Tony to have a drinking problem. That's because you don't have to be an alcoholic to have a drinking problem.

Sign Posts

Getting drunk, passing out, not remembering what you did, throwing up, and cringing in embarrassment aren't a normal part of social drinking. Neither is being arrested, getting in fights, having sex with someone you don't know or like, or wrecking your car.

If you drink, it's not too early to take a good look at the way you drink.

Because while there's a 90 percent chance that you won't become an alcoholic, odds are a lot better that you'll experience real problems if you drink irresponsibly.

Look at it this way: It doesn't matter much whether you were an alcoholic or just an unlucky "social drinker" if you end up getting scraped off a highway somewhere. You're just as dead either way. The same goes for getting pregnant, arrested, fired, humiliated in public, or your teeth punched in. Or simply losing your own self-respect.

> You don't have to be an alcoholic to have a drinking problem.

If you usually drink until you're drunk or if you often end up feeling guilty or embarrassed about things you do when drinking, or if drinking causes problems—even small problems—for you, then you're not a social drinker. And remember: You don't have to be an alcoholic to have a drinking problem.

If you're a careless drinker, do something about it now. Limit the amount you drink, drink slowly, don't drink and drive, don't drink and mix other drugs. Don't be embarrassed to turn down a drink or to ask for something other than alcohol. Don't take a drink to "be sociable" if you really don't want it.

If you try to limit how much you drink and fail, then you may be part of the 5.4 percent who become alcoholics. Don't forget that alcoholism takes a long time to develop, but problems can start early. The sooner you do something about a drinking problem, the less you—and the people you care about—will have to suffer.

Getting Help

If you're worried about your drinking and you haven't been able to cut back or control it on your own, help is nearby.

Check the phone book for an alcohol information center or treatment program. The people there can tell you where and how to get help. It's never too early—or too late—to start.

If you can't find an alcohol information center in your area, phone or write either (or both) of the following:

- The National Council on Alcoholism and Drug Dependence, 12 West 21st Street, New York, NY, 10010 (800) 622-2255
- Alcoholics Anonymous, P.O. Box 459, Grand Central Station, New York, NY 10163

Just do it—and do it now. There'll never be a better time to get your life back on track.

Here's looking at you—and at the person you can still become.

Point of Contention: Is Alcoholism a Disease?

In the past many people believed that alcoholics had weak morals and willpower. In 1957 the American Medical Association endorsed the concept that alcoholism is a disease—a medical condition (possibly inherited) that makes some individuals especially susceptible to alcohol. Some people still maintain that alcoholism is a behavior that alcoholics can choose to overcome, not a disease. Whether or not alcoholism is a disease has implications on how society views alcoholics and what methods of treatment should be pursued, as the two viewpoints below demonstrate.

Nicholas A. Pace is founder and medical director of Pace Medical Services and past president of the Alcoholism Center of Greater New York. Herbert Fingarette is a retired professor of philosophy at the University of California at Santa Barbara and author of *Heavy Drinking: The Myth of Alcoholism as a Disease.*

Alcoholism Is a Disease

Nicholas A. Pace

The medical community defines [alcoholism] as a disease. Back in the 1950s, the American Medical Association (AMA) indicated that alcoholism was a disease. In the August 26, 1992 issue of the *Journal of American Medical Association* (*JAMA*, Volume 68, Number 8), there is an updated definition of alcoholism. It says, *"The disease of al-coholism is a primary and chronic disease with genetic, psychosocial, and environmental factors influencing the development and manifestation. The disease is often pro-gressive and fatal. It is characterized by impaired control over drinking, preoccupation with drinking of alcohol, the use of alcohol despite adverse consequences, and distor-tions in thinking (most notably denial). Each of these symptoms may be continuous or periodic."* A simpler def-inition is "If alcohol is interfering in one's life—be it with his job, family, interpersonal relationships or health—he has the problem."

Unfortunately people still feel that alcoholism is a moral problem. It has nothing to do with morality; it is a medical problem. That's the way we should look at it. . . .

The Physical Effects of Alcoholism

A simpler medical definition of alcoholism is: *"Alcoholism is a chronic and fatal disease characterized by tolerance, physical dependence, and pathological organ changes."* I am treating a patient right now for his pancreatitis and a heart problem. He probably wouldn't have these problems if he hadn't suffered from the disease of alcoholism for so many years. Even though he has been through treatment, we are still seeing the medical consequences, and that's common.

The first thing I explain to my patients is about the me-tabolism of alcohol. Dr. Charles Lieber (the great liver spe-cialist from Mt. Sinai Hospital in New York) showed that when one develops alcoholism, the patient has a different way of breaking down alcohol. I think Dr. Lieber should get the Nobel Peace Prize for showing that alcoholics use a different metabolic pathway to break down alcohol, but he won't since alcoholism is stigmatized.

We know that 95% of alcohol is eliminated from the body by the liver, which breaks down the alcohol to carbon dioxide and water. A normal liver cell produces two main enzymes. One is called alcohol dehydrogenase (ADH), and it breaks the alcohol down to acetaldehyde, which is a poison. A good liver takes that acetaldehyde and, with the help of a second enzyme called aldehyde dehydrogenase (ALDH), further oxidizes it, breaking it down with a very complicated metabolic process called the Krebs cycle, to carbon dioxide and water. That's how the normal liver breaks down alcohol, and as long as this system is working there is no problem.

> Unfortunately people still feel that alcoholism is a moral problem. It has nothing to do with morality; it is a medical problem.

But of course occasionally a drinker overindulges. The next morning he has a hangover, for he has too much acetaldehyde in his system and not enough aldehyde dehydrogenase to get rid of it. So he feels the effects of the acetaldehyde on the brain, and it feels terrible, hence the hangover.

Charles Lieber demonstrated that when someone develops alcoholism, the nucleus of the liver cell produces an enzyme called Cytochrome p450 2E1. That enzyme allows the liver to metabolize the alcohol twice as fast but, in doing so, it produces a lot of the acetaldehyde, which is a cousin to formaldehyde and very toxic to the liver. There is not enough of that second enzyme, aldehyde dehydrogenase to continue the alcohol breakdown process.

Therefore, the alcoholic has a system allowing him or her to drink more than anybody else, while also producing a lot of this poison called acetaldehyde, of which they can't rid from their bodies. The microsomal system is the part of the liver cell that eliminates toxins. It goes haywire in the alcoholic so that their livers become less and less tolerant to alcohol. They have a deficient enzyme system, and that precedes the onset of alcoholism.

Patients need to understand that they have real metabolic defects causing their livers not to metabolize alcohol normally. When you lose this ability, you can't put it back. You can make a cucumber into a pickle, but you can't make the pickle back into the cucumber. . . .

Alcohol and the Brain

The other organ that is very, very involved with alcohol is the brain. We know that alcohol interferes with the electrical charges of neurons (or nerve cells), that send messages to the brain about thoughts, feelings, and learning. We know alcohol interferes with and alters neurotransmitters after chronic exposure and can also lead to atrophy, or brain shrinkage. We also know that advanced states of alcoholism cause states of dementia psychosis and that when tolerance increases, alcoholics exhibit signs of disorientation like paranoia and aggressiveness. . . .

Animal studies show that heavy alcohol intake depletes some of the brain's chemicals such as dopamine, gamma-aminobutyric and seratonin. These chemicals give us the feeling of well-being and pleasure. At the same time alcohol releases chemi-

> Alcoholism is a disease of denial.

cals that cause stress and depression. It's this chemical imbalance in the brain that may be responsible for alcoholism and its relapses.

But besides calling alcoholism a brain disease, it is more than that. Every major system in the body is affected. When someone gets drunk, it certainly interferes with his or her cerebellum. There are long-term effects on the nervous system. Liver and colon cancer are very rare primary cancers, but hepatoma is common in the alcoholic and recovering alcoholic. So alcoholism is a disease that affects not only the brain but also the liver, stomach, kidney, intestines, and pancreas. Impotence, infertility, muscle cramps, sleep disturbances, and cardiac arrhythmia are very common problems in the alcoholic.

> Patients need to understand that they have real metabolic defects causing their livers not to metabolize alcohol normally.

I have detoxified many alcoholics who were on medication for high blood pressure. When the alcohol is out of their systems, many times you find that they don't need medication to keep their blood pressure under control.

Alcoholism is the great masquerader. Years ago we used to say that syphilis was the great masquerader, but now you'd have to say alcohol is because it affects every system in the body from brain to bone marrow.

Excerpted from Nicholas A. Pace, interviewed by Kathy Petersen, "The Great Masquerader—Alcoholism," an online article found at www.lowefamily.org/interviews/oct99/htm. Reprinted with permission from the Lowe Family Foundation.

Alcoholism Is Not a Disease

Herbert Fingarette

The alcoholic is a tragic figure and deserves our compassion. But the idea that alcoholism is a disease is a harmful myth.

The slogan "alcoholism is a disease" sounds scientific.

But the public has not been told of the accumulated scientific evidence that by now clearly undermines almost all that slogan suggests, as well as the burgeoning treatment industry based on it.

Foremost is the idea that alcoholics, the victims of the supposed disease, suffer "loss of control" over drinking. In my book, *Heavy Drinking,* I described some of the many experiments and clinical reports, published in the mainstream research literature, that have demonstrated consistently that alcoholics can and do have a great deal of control over their drinking.

One of the most persistent of such myths propagated by the advocates of the disease concept of alcoholism is that if a sober alcoholic takes a first drink, the effect is to cause a physical inability to stop. This is unquestionably false. One sees this clearly in studies where alcoholics have been deceived about what they are drinking. Those who were in reality drinking alcohol, but were led to believe their beverage was non-alcoholic, made no effort to drink a lot of it. Certainly none drank uncontrollably, even after they had alcohol in their system.

Alcoholics Can Stop Drinking

The point is that it is not the chemical effect of alcohol that triggers the drinking. It is things like the particular social setting, the stresses of job or family, the belief that they are "alcoholics" and "have" to drink.

> The idea that alcoholism is a disease is a harmful myth.

Ironically, the so-called "treatment programs" for the "disease of alcoholism" provide overwhelming proof that alcoholics do have control. Almost all treatment methods of dealing with this so-called disease, whether they are "medical" or of the Alcoholics Anonymous type, immediately confront the alcoholic with this proposition: To enter this program you must take responsibility for the way you're living. You can and you must stop drinking at once, and you must remain abstinent voluntarily. What's more, the patients do it. Because now they want to. Of course this would be impossible if the drinking were actually caused by some physical or other uncontrollable process in the alcoholic's body.

Still, one might ask: Regardless of the inconsistency, isn't the bottom line that these treatments are effective? The truth, unfortunately, is that they are not. They are largely waste. Yet we are paying out over a billion dollars a year—financed largely by taxes and higher insurance premiums for all—in order to sup port a proliferation of public and private alcoholism clinics that are known to be largely failures.

A shocking accusation? Yet at least half a dozen independent studies, by leading scientific authorities here and abroad, as well as the 1983 comprehensive report to the U.S. Congress, tell us again and again that these programs contribute little or nothing to the improvement of their patients. The programs, of course, report that a substantial proportion of their patients leave the program much improved. Are they lying? Not at all.

Don't Reward Heavy Drinking
What the public is not told is that the rates of improvement for similar persons who do not go through treatment is about the same. The programs contribute nothing additional. What counts is motivation plus things like educational level, job status, and family status.

Another of the prevalent ideas fostered by the advocates of the disease concept of alcoholism is that it is genetically caused—which is a harmful half-truth. The full truth, reported in the data of the geneticists themselves, is that the role of genes seems real but quite limited. For example, the major genetic study by Dr. Robert Cloninger and his associates concluded: "Major changes in social attitudes about drinking styles can change dramatically the prevalence of alcohol abuse regardless of genetic predisposition." In short, you can't blame it on the genes; your life is in your own hands.

The unspoken but real significance of the "disease" notion is not medical but economic and political. Once the "disease" label is accepted widely as applying to some human problem, it becomes a license for health professionals to assume authority and to expand their practice.

Sometimes that is justified. Not here, though. It has become a legal basis for arguing that heavy drinkers should be excused from legal and moral responsibilities for any misdeeds. It has been used to justify providing them increasingly with special government and insurance benefits. We are told this is compassion. And it would be, if the money spent for "treatment" got results. It would be compassion if it encouraged alcohol abusers to stop, whereas in reality the benefits are *rewards* for heavy drinking, and the excuses *encourage* evasion of responsibility.

Why is there such resistance to public challenge of this doctrine? I do not ascribe malicious motives to the alcoholism treatment personnel if I point out that when tens of thousands of careers and billions of dollars are at stake, it is contrary to human nature to expect disinterested openness to new evidence. And those many alcoholics who have been emotionally indoctrinated join in resisting bitterly the public exposure of a doctrine to which they have a kind of religious commitment.

In reporting this evidence to the public, my objective has not been to heap blame on alcoholics. Far from it. We ought to have compassion for these people who have gradually, unwittingly, over years got themselves increasingly tangled up in a tragically destructive way of life. But help begins by confronting the alcoholic with the truth, not with the evasion that it is a "disease" that has taken over the alcoholic's will.

We should offer them our best counsel, and our moral support. But they must also face the fact that no one can do the job for them. They have to take their lives in their hands and change the way they live. Many alcoholics do responsibly fight their way to a better way of life. This is where the evidence now points, and where hope lies.

Excerpted from Herbert Fingarette, " The Alcoholism Debate: Disease or Not," *The San Diego Union-Tribune*, January 29, 1989. Reprinted with permission from the author.

Chapter 3

Alcohol, Driving, and the Law

Zero Tolerance for Alcohol

The Century Council

The Century Council, an alcohol awareness organization, provides two reasons why teenagers should think twice before drinking and driving. The first is that alcohol greatly increases your chances of being in a car accident. Such accidents are a leading cause of death for people between the ages of 15 and 20. A second reason is the risk of losing your driver's license. Most states have passed laws that revoke the license of drivers under 21 found to have any alcohol in their system.

Motor vehicle crashes are the leading cause of death for young people 15 to 20 years of age. In 1998, 21 percent of the young drivers who were killed in crashes were intoxicated. While alcohol-related fatalities for youth under 21 have declined by 57 percent between 1982 and 1998, non-alcohol-related fatalities for youth have increased almost 10 percent. There remains much to be done to continue to reduce deaths and injuries to our young people—both alcohol- and non-alcohol-related.

For underage persons, the effects of alcohol in combination with novice level driving skills can be a deadly combination.

Reprinted from "Zero Tolerance Position Paper," by The Century Council (www. centurycouncil.org), April 1999. Reprinted with permission.

Full compliance with a Zero Tolerance law means if a person under the age of 21 drives with a BAC [blood alcohol concentration] level of .02 or higher (compared to the adult level of .08 or .10), he/she will be considered to be in violation of the law.

Various studies agree that young drivers who have been drinking have a greater risk of involvement in fatal crashes than adults with similar BAC levels. The *Journal of Studies of Alcohol* reports that young drivers with BACs of .05 to .10 are far more likely to be killed in single vehicle crashes than sober young drivers. The relative risk of fatal crash involvement is substantially higher for drivers under age 21 at lower BAC levels than for drivers age 25 or older. According to NHTSA [the National Highway Traffic and Safety Administration], male drivers age 16 to 20 have six times the driver fatality risk in single vehicle crashes at BACs of .01 to .04 compared to male drivers age 25 and older at these low levels.

Zero Tolerance blood alcohol concentration, especially when

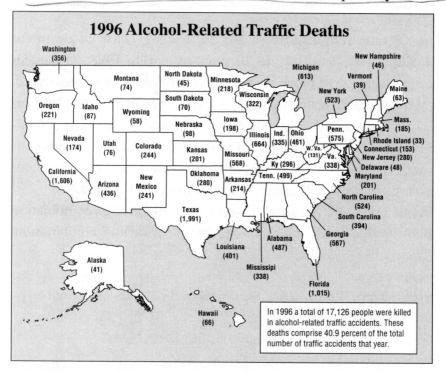

1996 Alcohol-Related Traffic Deaths

Washington (356)
Oregon (221)
Idaho (87)
Montana (74)
Nevada (174)
Utah (76)
Wyoming (58)
California (1,606)
Arizona (436)
New Mexico (241)
Colorado (244)
North Dakota (45)
South Dakota (70)
Nebraska (98)
Kansas (201)
Oklahoma (280)
Texas (1,991)
Minnesota (218)
Iowa (198)
Missouri (568)
Arkansas (214)
Louisiana (401)
Wisconsin (322)
Illinois (664)
Michigan (613)
Ind. (335)
Ohio (461)
Ky (296)
Tenn. (499)
Mississipi (338)
Alabama (487)
New York (523)
Penn. (575)
W. Va. (131)
Va. (338)
New Hampshire (46)
Vermont (39)
Maine (63)
Mass. (185)
Rhode Island (33)
Connecticut (153)
New Jersey (280)
Delaware (48)
Maryland (201)
North Carolina (524)
South Carolina (394)
Georgia (567)
Florida (1,015)
Alaska (41)
Hawaii (66)

In 1996 a total of 17,126 people were killed in alcohol-related traffic accidents. These deaths comprise 40.9 percent of the total number of traffic accidents that year.

coupled with Administrative License Revocation (ALR), acts as an effective deterrent for young people who consider drinking and driving. When coupled, these laws require the automatic suspension of a driver's license when that driver refuses to take a breath or blood analysis test, or if the result of the test measures over the level set for drivers under 21.

> For underage persons, the effects of alcohol in combination with novice level driving skills can be a deadly combination.

Two studies attest to the fact that those two measures combine to have an important impact of alcohol-related injury and fatality data for young drivers.

Subsequent to the state of Maryland's enactment of an underage Zero Tolerance BAC-ALR law, alcohol-related crashes dropped 11 percent. The reduction jumped to 50 percent in test counties where a public education campaign dedicated to informing young drivers about the law was carried out.

A second study published in *Public Health Reports* cited, on average, a 20 percent reduction in single vehicle night time fatal crashes occurred among adolescents based on data from the first 12 states to enact lower BAC laws for minors.

Establishing a lower BAC for drivers under 21 does not unfairly discriminate against young people. The evidence clearly suggests that young people who drink and drive are far more dangerous to others and themselves than sober youthful drivers and adult drivers who drive after drinking. Further, a national poll showed that 90 percent of youths with licenses said the certain threat of losing them on-the-spot would strongly deter them from drinking and driving.

As of June, 1998, all 50 states and the District of Columbia have enacted Zero Tolerance laws establishing a BAC limit of .02 or lower for drivers under the age of 21. Additionally all states have 21 year old minimum drinking age laws.

The Tragic Results of Drinking and Driving— Two Stories

Janice Arenofsky

Drunk driving has caused countless tragedies. Journalist Janice Arenofsky describes two young women's personal experiences involving alcohol and driving. Kimberly accidentally killed a bicyclist and was sentenced to a year in jail for involuntary manslaughter. Maureen never had an accident, but her arrest for drunk driving forced her to confront her drinking problem.

In 1997, more than 16,000 people—including approximately 2,200 young adults ages 15 to 20—were killed in álcohol-related crashes, reports MADD (Mothers Against Drunk Driving).

Not every drinking and driving incident ends with a death, but the risk increases dramatically when alcohol is part of the picture. The lives of these two young women make that point.

Kimberly's Story

Kimberly Bowers, from Phoenix, Arizona, is now 21. In April 1997, Kimberly, then a freshman broadcasting student at Arizona State University (ASU), drove drunk and killed Alex, a 26-

Reprinted from Janice Arenofsky, "I'll Never Drink and Drive Again," *Current Health*, vol. 26, no. 4, December 1999. Reprinted with permission from Weekly Reader Corporation.

year-old bicyclist. This is her story:

"One night, after a few fraternity parties at which I'd had around six beers, my friend and I decided to take a drive and talk about his girlfriend problems. I hadn't had a drink for an hour, so I thought I'd be OK to drive.

> Not every drinking and driving incident ends with a death, but the risk increases dramatically when alcohol is part of the picture.

"It was about 3 a.m., and I was in the right-hand lane of a street near the ASU campus. I was going within the speed limit. I didn't see anyone, but suddenly I heard the windshield shatter. So I doubled back to see what had happened.

"I saw a bicycle and a guy lying in the road with doughnuts scattered around him. We tried to talk to him, but then I really started freaking out. I only had a few minor cuts.

"The police gave me a breathalyzer test, then took me to the hospital for a blood test. I spent that night in jail, where I called my dad. Until then I'd been in shock, but I really broke down then. I knew my life was going to be changed forever.

"I was legally intoxicated with a BAC [blood alcohol concentration] of .108. I was found guilty of involuntary manslaughter. I hoped for a plea bargain, but the judge sentenced me to a year in jail in 'tent city.' I worked in the laundry there and lived with 180 other women in tents. I had to put up with fights, terrible food, unfriendly guards, no privacy, and extremely venomous brown recluse spiders. After nine months, the judge released me on probation (until February 2000) so I could talk to high school audiences and other youth groups about my drinking/driving experience.

"Before the accident, I never considered myself an alcoholic, but now I think I might have been heading in that direction. I also used to think I drove better when I was drunk—that my senses were heightened. The scary part is I know I've been even more intoxicated than I was that night and I still would drive. I'll never drink and drive again. That's for sure.

"Since I became a felon, I lost my college scholarship. And it's hard to find a job to help pay for my community college tuition. I also had my driver's license suspended for four years, until 2001.

"I thought this would never happen to me, but I don't take anything for granted anymore. Take that taxi home. It's that simple."

Maureen's Story

Although death and jail are not part of Maureen's personal story, the 22-year-old says they might have been.

"I started using alcohol when I was 13. On weekends I'd hang out and drink at different kids' houses when the parents were away. By age 16, I drank almost every day. I'd sometimes cut school to drink, but mostly I drank at night. My grades went down, and eventually I was kicked out of school.

"By the time I got my driver's license, I was drinking every day to get drunk. Usually when I was driving at night, I'd either be drunk or on some other drug. I remember once driving home from a party when the passenger had to help me stay between the white lines. It was a good five miles. Another time I drove home alone from the New Jersey shore, and I have no recollection of the experience. I drove at least 10 times with blackouts.

> Before the accident, I never considered myself an alcoholic, but now I think I might have been heading in that direction.

"When I drove I felt invincible, so I often speeded. Once I partied and a couple of hours later was in a driving accident. A guy came out of a side street and hit me on the passenger door. The cops said it was no one's fault, but I think my reflexes were slow. I didn't see him until he hit me.

"Although I never got a DUI [driving under the influence] or DWI [driving while intoxicated], there were many times when I never should have been driving. I was just lucky that I didn't hurt myself or anyone else.

"Because I wasn't falling-down drunk, I didn't realize my condition. I just wanted to get into the car and get somewhere. And so did my passengers. They didn't care if I got into an accident or got pulled over because it would be me getting the ticket, not them. And no one worried about getting hurt or injuring anyone. It never occurred to us.

"Finally, I got arrested. At age 20, I was sent to a halfway house where I stopped drinking and realized I had screwed up my life because of alcohol.

"Today I don't drink. But every time I get on the road, I worry about how many other teens are doing what I used to do—drinking and driving. I worry especially around the holidays.

"Since I'm sober, life is a hundred times better than it was when I was drinking. Because when you're drinking, you're not [really experiencing] life."

State Penalties for Underage Drinking

Ohio Department of Public Safety

Many states have passed alcohol and driving laws aimed specifically at teens. Presented below are some of the laws of the state of Ohio. Teenagers in Ohio convicted of operating a motor vehicle with at least a .02 percent blood alcohol concentration can have their licenses suspended and be compelled to participate in an alcohol addiction program. Those found using a false I.D. to purchase alcohol face mandatory fines and jail time. Parents who allow underage consumption of alcohol can be prosecuted and/or sued.

Consequences of Under 21 Drinking

Law enforcement officers can file charges against any driver under 21 who has a blood alcohol concentration (BAC) of at least .02% but less than .10%. If convicted of operating a motor vehicle after underage consumption (OMVUAC):

- you can face a 60-day and not more than two-year license suspension.
- the courts may also commit you to as many as three days in a certified alcohol and drug addiction program.
- 4 points will be assessed to your driving record.

Reprinted from "The Facts of Underage Drinking," by the Ohio Department of Public Safety (www.state.oh.us). Reprinted with permission.

• a remedial driving course must be completed before your driver's license will be reissued. The remedial driving course is required to devote a number of hours to instruction in the area of alcohol and drugs in the operation of a motor vehicle.

Using a Fake I.D. to Purchase Alcohol

A person under the age of 21 who presents a false, fictitious, or altered I.D. or driver's license when purchasing beer or liquor

Estimated Lives Saved by Minimum Drinking Age Laws (MDAs)

Year	Lives Saved	Cumulative Lives Saved by MDA's since 1982
1982	578	578
1983	609	1,187
1984	709	1,896
1985	701	2,597
1986	840	3,437
1987	1,071	4,508
1988	1,148	5,656
1989	1,093	6,749
1990	1,033	7,782
1991	941	8,723
1992	795	9,518
1993	816	10,334
1994	848	11,182
1995	851	12,033
1996	846	12,879
1997	846	13,725
1998	861	14,586

MADD and the National Highway Traffic and Safety Administration.

shall receive the following penalties:

- First Offense—*Mandatory* fine of $250–$1,000 and jail time up to six months.
- Second Offense—*Mandatory* fine of $500–$1,000 and jail time up to six months and possible license suspension up to 60 days.
- Third and Subsequent Offenses—*Mandatory* fine of $500–$1,000 and jail time up to six months. 90-day license suspension with an option of community service and a license suspension until age 21.

What Parents Should Know

- You cannot give alcohol to your children's friends under 21 years of age under any circumstances, even in your own home, even with their parent's permission.
  - You cannot knowingly allow a person under 21 to remain in your home or on your property while consuming or possessing alcoholic beverages.

If You Break the Law

- you can face a maximum sentence of six months in jail and/or a $1,000 fine.
- Officers can take any alcohol, money or property used in committing this offense (glasses, musical equipment, refrigerator, furniture). *YOU MAY NOT GET IT BACK!*
- Others can sue you if you give alcohol to anyone under 21 and they, in turn, hurt someone or damage property. . . .

REMEMBER! Alcohol-related crashes are the leading cause of teenage deaths. Parents' attitudes and behaviors about alcohol influence the attitudes and behaviors of their children.

Injured by a Drunk Driver

Lisa Wright

Drunk drivers are not just a threat to themselves. Riding as a passenger in a car with an alcohol-impaired driver is just as dangerous. Lisa Wright describes below how during her senior year in high school she suffered permanent injuries when the car she and her friends were in crashed; everyone, including the driver, had been drinking. She urges others to learn from her mistakes.

I wasn't the perfect 17-year-old high school senior, but I was pretty normal. I was a cheerleader and the president of my class in Birch Run, Michigan. I was a good student. I had a lot going for me, and I was really looking forward to college.

I drank, but I wasn't the kind of person who was out drinking all the time or even every weekend. I just liked to party with my friends and have a good time. Sometimes, like a lot of kids, I did get drunk.

Joe was my boyfriend at the time. He was the kind of person who would often drink and drive. Even though I never drove drunk, I rode with him pretty often when he had been drinking, and it always seemed that everything would be OK.

He lived about an hour away, and one weekend he came up

Reprinted from Lisa Wright, "Lisa's Story," *Current Health*, vol. 24, no. 6, February 1997. Reprinted with permission from Weekly Reader Corporation.

with some friends I had never met before. My girlfriend and I went driving with them, and we couldn't figure out what we wanted to do.

Joe had a fake ID and bought some vodka and wine coolers. The truth is Joe and his friends had been drinking before they even arrived at my house. I could smell it on Joe's breath, but I wasn't worried. It wasn't the first time. Pretty soon we all were drinking and cruising around. It got later and later, too late to really do anything like go to the movies. So we just kept drinking and cruising. We ended up about an hour and a half from my town. I think we were looking for a place to play pool or something.

Joe gave up the driver's seat to a guy named Jason. I remember sitting in the back seat on Joe's lap while Jason drove, and I recall that nobody was wearing a seat belt.

After that, I don't remember anything. The police report says that Jason took a curve in a 25 mph zone at somewhere between 80 and 90 mph. The car went off the road, hit a telephone pole, and flipped four times before stopping in a driveway.

Amazingly, nobody else was seriously hurt. But I was hurt badly—thrown straight through the back window. I was rushed to the trauma unit, and for several days the doctors didn't know if I was going to live. My lungs were badly damaged; that was the main concern. After five days or so, it was clear that I would live.

> The car went off the road, hit a telephone pole, and flipped four times. . . . I was . . . thrown straight through the back window.

But I was in such bad shape. I had broken a bunch of bones: my shoulder blades, my collar bone, my jaw, five of my ribs. I don't remember realizing I couldn't feel my legs. I was on so many drugs that everything seemed like a blur. It took a couple of weeks to get my head straight. Still, I do remember something was terribly wrong. I asked the doctor if I would be able to walk again, and he just looked at me and said no. I remember how cold he was. He didn't try to make it seem better than it was, and I'm glad. He made me open my eyes and face facts.

One day, a few weeks after the accident, I looked in the mirror and thought, "Oh, God, I'm a monster. I look like such a freak." I had scars on my face; my eyes were completely red.

> When alcohol is involved, tragedy can be right around the next corner.

You couldn't even see the whites of my eyes. My face was swollen, my teeth had huge braces on them, and I didn't even remember the surgery on my mouth. They put a hole in my throat so I could breathe. I had tubes up my nose. It was pretty gross—and terribly painful.

For a while I thought about killing myself, but I was too sick to do anything about it. I thought my life was completely over. I thought there is no way I'm ever going to make it out of this. No one is ever going to love me. I'll never be able to get married and have kids. I thought this just can't be happening. It's not me. But it was me.

Putting things back together took a long, long time. I went to a rehabilitation center in Colorado. It was really hard, and I was in a lot of pain. I had no idea what was in store for me. Learning to do the simplest things like getting dressed or putting on a pair of shoes was exhausting. In fact, I was so weak that just sitting up could make me so dizzy that I'd vomit.

In Colorado, I was miserable. I cried every day. Joe and I broke up, and that was pretty terrible. But I wanted to go home so much that I kept working super hard, lifting weights, stretching, learning to become mobile in my wheelchair. I went home after three months, even though they wanted me to stay for another month. I made it home for graduation and the senior prom.

When the thrill of returning home wore off, I felt like a stranger in my own house—like I was living someone else's life. I couldn't do a lot of things I wanted to, and I realized that three months of rehab was just the beginning.

Slowly things have gotten better. My parents and close friends have always been there for me. It's now a year and a half since the accident. I've just finished my first year of college, and I'm really excited about getting my own specially equipped van so I can drive myself. I'll be able to live on my own and take care of myself completely without having to rely on anyone else. I'm fortunate enough to have the use of my hands. There are a lot of people who can't say that.

But the truth is I'm still working to be independent. I struggle with it every day. For example, I have a boyfriend, and when I'm out somewhere (I'm always in my wheelchair), a lot of times people stare at me. That really gets him mad, but I'm learning to ignore it. In fact, most of the time I don't even realize people are staring.

Of course, there's nothing in the world I would want more than to be able to walk again. And yet, a lot of good has come out of all this. Before, I didn't really appreciate what I had. I took a lot of things and people for granted. Now, I've gained a lot of compassion for people. I appreciate life a lot more than I used to. In fact, I can't remember being this happy before.

If I could give advice to anyone about alcohol and driving, I'd say don't drink and drive—and *never* get in a car with someone who has been drinking. You just can't make exceptions. People think that the possibility of being in an accident is so far away— that tragedy is so distant. But when alcohol is involved, tragedy can be right around the next corner.

Point of Contention: Are Age-21 Laws Effective in Reducing Alcohol Abuse Among Teens?

In France, Belgium, Germany, and Italy, it is legal for 16-year-olds to drink alcohol. Some countries, such as Spain and New Zealand, allow even younger children to drink in public in the company of their parents. In the United States, however, it is illegal for persons under 21 to purchase or publicly consume alcoholic beverages. Some parents in the United States feel that prohibiting alcohol ensures that teens do not learn how to consume it responsibly. In their view, parents should teach their children the principles of safe drinking and allow them to consume some alcohol before they are 21, as many Europeans do. On the other hand, many parents believe that age-21 drinking laws should be strictly enforced in order to protect teenagers from the harmful consequences of alcohol abuse.

Two parents of teens reflect these opposing approaches to underage drinking. Barbara Bennett is an Arlington, Texas, resident who helped organize a community program in which parents sign pledges agreeing to chaperone parties and not to supply alcohol to teens. Elizabeth M. Whelan is a public health scientist and president of the American Council of Science and Health.

Laws Against Underage Drinking Should Be More Strictly Enforced

Barbara Bennett

Even as a child I envisioned myself as mature, grownup, and wise beyond my years. Most children feel that way. Of course, few actually are. Just little boys and little girls learning to cope with life. Nothing more, nothing less.

Increasingly we live in a world that no longer sees a need to protect its children. At earlier and earlier ages they are given the latitude to make what are in truth "adult decisions." Take, for example, the choice of whether to drink. Currently, in this country we have over three million underage alcoholics. Three million. In truth, young people become addicted five to 10 times faster than a grown adult. An additional 20 percent of this group are problem drinkers, though non-addicts.

Parents Are Part of the Problem

Sadly, those who should be part of the solution, often are part of the problem. I know parents who allow alcohol parties on their property and some who even go as far as to provide the booze. They make excuses like "It's only beer." Or maybe, "I always take the keys." My personal favorite is "I'd rather see them drink here than someplace else." This illegal activity sound familiar to any of you?

Twelve is the average age of drinking onset, not the lawful 21. Indulge me a moment. Statistically speaking, for each child that begins to imbibe at 16, some 8-year-old is sipping his first beer. Both are four years from the average. Sixteen plus eight, divided by two makes twelve. That's how it works. If more waited until legal age, the average would be higher. Few do, and there is the problem.

About seven years ago, when my oldest daughter was 14, I hosted a non-alcoholic New Year's Eve party. All went well until shortly after midnight. At the corner of our property some older teens from across the street had come over and blatantly offered the ninth-graders beer. Our guests had to be ushered back into the house. I wasn't pleased. When I called the parent who sponsored the other party the next morning to complain, she informed me I needed to get in the "real" world. Times have not gotten any easier.

My babies are now 19 and 21. Many of you are just getting started. Remember, a 10-year-old driving a car and a 15-year-old drinking are both equal distances from legal. Alcohol—not a choice till 21. That's the law. With drinking there is no knowledge or test requirement that you demonstrate you can handle alcohol before you get behind a bottle or can, either. Now there is an idea worth exploring. Maybe we should require a drinking license? Legislators are you listening?

The National Center on Addiction and Substance Abuse at Columbia University states, "A child who reaches 21 without using drugs, smoking cigarettes or abusing alcohol is virtually certain never to do so." I believe that. Several years back I informally asked about a dozen providers of adult alcohol treatment this question: "How many of your patients waited until 21 to start drinking?" One remembered a woman who did not drink until 30, but none of the others could recall a single patient. Interesting.

The No. 1 Drug Problem
Alcohol is the No. 1 drug problem in the United States. It is also proven a strong gateway drug to other substance

abuses. Marijuana . . . cocaine . . . heroin. If we could seriously curb underage drinking, we would realistically change the face of this country. It's true. I once had a police chief tell me, "If it wasn't for alcohol, I'd be out of a job." Nationally, just with *teens,* alcohol is involved in almost ninety thousand auto accidents a year, nearly 4,000 fatal crashes, four out of five suicide attempts, 85 percent of teen pregnancies, half of all rapes, and virtually every date rape. Sure makes you think. What if no one drank until 21?

> Young people become addicted five to 10 times faster than a grown adult.

Poisoning, and even death from alcohol overdoses have become increasingly common. In the past 10 years the dangerous practice of binge drinking on the college campus has doubled, and high school students' consumption reflects the same trend. Today, we aren't talking about a shared beer behind the tool shed with a buddy. We are talking volume. When a parent of the turbulent '60s has to think of her high school years as the "good ol' days," maybe it is time we woke up to the facts of the now. "Toto, we aren't in Kansas anymore."

In my hometown of Miami, Florida, everything imaginable was available, but was simply not tolerated as a teen choice. Unofficially, our senior class motto was "sin, sex, wine . . . we're the class of '69." Thankfully we were more bark than bite. Few parties I attended even had a hint of alcohol or other drugs, and none openly. One night a guy did show up drunk at a birthday bash and did "wheelies" on his motorcycle in my back yard. Then there were the varsity cheerleaders who went on a road trip with the team and got busted for drinking. They were thrown off the squad. No one sued. No one thought it unfair. Everyone was angry with the students. Weird concept. The school felt dishonored and the girls' parents were mortified. Things have changed.

Drinking Is a Choice

Today parents get lawyers. The question is no longer applied consequences, but denied consequences. How do we get them off? Leaving your homework on the kitchen table, or spilling a soda at lunch is a mistake. Underage drinking is not a mistake! Illegal alcohol consumption is an intentional choice. Stupid, but intentional.

> Underage drinking is not a mistake! Illegal alcohol consumption is an intentional choice.

As a society, we need to fight for the return of our children. Where have they all gone? Here's a thought. Maybe if more adults acted like adults, then kids would be free to be kids. Growing up too fast frequently results in not growing up at all. Please, help save our children.

Reprinted from Barbara Bennett, "Where Have All the Children Gone?" *Arlington Morning News*, November 26, 1999. Reprinted with permission from the author.

Perils of Prohibition: Why We Should Lower the Drinking Age to 18

Elizabeth M. Whelan

My colleagues at the Harvard School of Public Health, where I studied preventive medicine, deserve high praise for their recent study on teenage drinking. What they found in their survey of college students was that they drink "early and . . . often," frequently to the point of getting ill.

As a public-health scientist with a daughter, Christine, heading to college this fall, I have professional and personal concerns about teen binge drinking. It is imperative that we explore *why* so many young people abuse alcohol. From my own study of the effects of alcohol restrictions and my observations of Christine and her friends' predicament about drinking, I believe that today's laws are unrealistic. Prohibiting the sale of liquor to responsible young adults creates an atmosphere where binge drinking and alcohol abuse have become a problem. American teens, unlike their European peers, don't learn how to drink gradually, safely and in moderation.

Alcohol is widely accepted and enjoyed in our culture. Studies show that moderate drinking can be good for you. But we legally proscribe alcohol until the age of 21 (why not 30 or 45?). Christine and her classmates can drive cars, fly planes, marry, vote, pay taxes, take out loans and risk their lives as members of the U.S. armed forces. But laws in all 50 states say that no alcoholic beverages may be sold to anyone until that magic 21st birthday. We didn't always have a national "21" rule. When I was in college, in the mid-'60s, the drinking age varied from state to state. This posed its own risks, with underage students crossing state lines to get a legal drink.

In parts of the Western world, moderate drinking by teenagers and even children under their parents' supervision is a given. Though the per capita consumption of alcohol in France, Spain and Portugal is higher than in the United States, the rate of alcoholism and alcohol abuse is lower. A glass of wine at dinner is normal practice. Kids learn to regard moderate drinking as an enjoyable family activity rather than as something they have to sneak away to do. Banning drinking by young people makes it a badge of adulthood—a tantalizing forbidden fruit.

Christine and her teenage friends like to go out with a group to a club, comedy show or sports bar to watch the game. But teens today have to go on the sly with fake IDs and the fear of getting caught. Otherwise, they're denied admittance to most places and left to hang out on the street. That's hardly a safer alternative. Christine and her classmates now find themselves in a legal no man's land. At 18, they're considered adults. Yet when they want to enjoy a drink like other adults, they are, as they put it, "disenfranchised."

Comparing my daughter's dilemma with my own as an "underage" college student, I see a difference—and one that I think has exacerbated the current dilemma. Today's teens are far more sophisticated than we were. They're treated less like children and have more responsibilities than we did. This makes the 21 restriction seem anachronistic.

For the past few years, my husband and I have been preparing Christine for college life and the inevitable partying—read keg of beer—that goes with it. Last year, a young friend with no drinking experience was violently ill for days after he was introduced to "clear liquids in small glasses" during freshman orientation. We want our daughter to learn how to drink sensibly and avoid this pitfall. Starting at the age of 14, we invited her to join us for a glass of champagne with dinner. She'd tried it once before, thought it was "yucky" and declined. A year later, she enjoyed sampling wine at family meals.

> Prohibiting the sale of liquor to responsible young adults creates an atmosphere where binge drinking and alcohol abuse have become a problem.

When, at 16, she asked for a Mudslide (a bottled chocolate-milk-and-rum concoction), we used the opportunity to discuss it with her. We explained the alcohol content, told her the alcohol level is lower when the drink is blended with ice and compared it with a glass of wine. Since the drink of choice on campus is beer, we contrasted its potency with wine and hard liquor and stressed the importance of not drinking on an empty stomach.

> We should make access to alcohol legal at 18.

Our purpose was to encourage her to know the alcohol content of what she is served. We want her to experience the effects of liquor in her own home, not on the highway and not for the first time during a college orientation week with free-flowing suds. Although Christine doesn't drive yet, we regularly reinforce the concept of choosing a designated driver. Happily, that already seems a widely accepted practice among our daughter's friends who drink.

We recently visited the Ivy League school Christine will attend in the fall. While we were there, we read a story in the college paper about a student who was nearly electrocuted when, in a drunken state, he climbed on top of a moving train at a railroad station near the campus. The student survived, but three of his limbs were later amputated. This incident reminded me of a tragic death on another campus. An intoxicated student maneuvered himself into a chimney. He was found three days later when frat brothers tried to light a fire in the fireplace. By then he was dead.

These tragedies are just two examples of our failure to teach young people how to use alcohol prudently. If 18-year-olds don't have legal access to even a beer at a public place, they have no experience handling liquor on their own. They feel "liberated" when they arrive on campus.

With no parents to stop them, they have a "let's make up for lost time" attitude. The result: binge drinking.

We should make access to alcohol legal at 18. At the same time, we should come down much harder on alcohol abusers and drunk drivers of all ages. We should intensify our efforts at alcohol education for adolescents. We want them to understand that it is perfectly OK not to drink. But if they do, alcohol should be consumed in moderation.

After all, we choose to teach our children about safe sex, including the benefits of teen abstinence. Why, then, can't we—schools and parents alike—teach them about safe drinking?

Reprinted from Elizabeth M. Whelan, "Perils of Prohibition," *Newsweek*, May 29, 1995. All rights reserved. Reprinted with permission.

Chapter 4

When Someone You Know Has a Drinking Problem

A Guide to Helping Friends Who Abuse Alcohol or Drugs

Betsy O'Connor

Even if you choose not to drink or do not have a problem with alcohol, you might have a friend who does. How can a person tell if someone has a drinking or drug problem? How serious can it be? What can friends do to help? Below, these and other questions are answered by Betsy O'Connor, an alcoholism counselor. She describes warning signs that may indicate a serious substance abuse problem and provides guidelines for discussing the issue with problem drinkers.

How can I tell if my friend has a drinking or other drug problem?

Sometimes it's tough to tell. Most kids won't walk up to someone they're close to and ask for help. In fact, your friend will probably do everything possible to deny or hide the problem. But, there are signs you can look for. People with serious substance abuse problems say things like, "I can stop drinking or using other drugs any time I want to"—but they don't. They may be o.k. to hang around with, until they get high—then they

Excerpted from Betsy O'Connor, *A Guide for Teens.* A brochure published by the Center for Health Communication of the Harvard School of Public Health, 1994. Reprinted with permission.

often act like jerks or get into fights. No one is sure why some people get into trouble with alcohol or other drugs. There are signs, however, when substances are taking control of someone's life. Some of these signs are easy to see, others aren't, but if you see them happening over and over again, chances are your friend needs help.

Warning Signs

If your friend has one or more of the following warning signs, he or she may have a problem with alcohol or other drugs:

- getting drunk or high on drugs on a regular basis
- lying about things, or about how much alcohol or other drugs he or she is using
- avoiding you in order to get drunk or high
- giving up activities he or she used to do, such as sports, homework, or hanging out with friends who don't drink or use other drugs
- planning drinking in advance, hiding alcohol, drinking or using other drugs alone
- having to drink more to get the same high
- believing that in order to have fun you need to drink or use other drugs
- frequent hangovers
- pressuring others to drink or use other drugs
- taking risks, including sexual risks
- having "blackouts"—forgetting what he or she did the night before while drinking (if you tell your friend what happened, he or she might pretend to remember, or laugh it off as no big deal)
- feeling run-down, hopeless, depressed, or even suicidal
- sounding selfish and not caring about others
- constantly talking about drinking or using other drugs
- getting in trouble with the law
- drinking and driving

- suspension from school for an alcohol- or other drug-related incident

How serious can my friend's drinking or other drug problem be? What can it lead to?

Not all people who drink or use other drugs develop the same symptoms or consequences, but one thing is for sure: If your friend has a drinking or other drug problem and doesn't get help, things can get much worse. People with serious drinking or other drug problems don't like to admit it, even to themselves. In the beginning, they often say they feel great, that drinking or smoking pot or doing a few lines of cocaine is the best thing that ever happened to them. But then things change for the worse. Eventually, if they don't get help, they can develop serious psychological problems such as suicidal depression, and serious physical problems such as liver damage and brain damage; and some will die from an overdose. Getting drunk or high impairs judgment, and may lead to behaviors that people wouldn't do ordinarily if they weren't under the influence of these substances—such as having unsafe sex which could result in pregnancy, AIDS, or other sexually transmitted diseases. Substance abuse is dangerous; it can ruin your friend's health, cause your friend to drop out of school, lose friends, lose values, and even lose his or her self-respect.

> If your friend has a drinking or other drug problem and doesn't get help, things can get much worse.

Alcohol and other drugs don't care who you are, what color you are, if you're rich or poor, how old you are, your sex, or where you're from. They don't care if you're a jock, a cheerleader, or a genius.

What would cause my friend to have a serious drinking or other drug problem?

Lots of things lead to these problems. For one thing, these difficulties often run in families, just like heart disease and cancer.

If your friend's parents are alcoholic, or there is a family history of alcoholism or other drug addiction, your friend is more

---

Family Intervention

The power of an intervention comes from having the participants express concern and compassion for the alcoholic's welfare, said Mary McMahon, an intervention specialist for Intervention Services, Inc., in Edina, Minn. McMahon has family members and friends write letters to the alcoholic and then read them aloud at the intervention. The letters allow family members to express their feelings without threatening or blaming the chemically dependent person.

"A family member might say, 'I love you and I care about you, but I'm concerned. These are the things I see happening to you,'" McMahon said. "Then I have each person tie their own feelings to the statements. They might give examples of times they were hurt by the alcoholic. For instance, a child may write, 'You went to my basketball game and everybody knew you had been drinking; I was so embarrassed.'". . .

McMahon offers a few guidelines for people considering intervention:

• Participants need to be educated about the disease of chemical dependency prior to the intervention. Their letters should be concise, well rehearsed, and should accentuate the positive.

• Interventions should take place on neutral territory.

• People invited to the intervention should include family members, close friends, and, when appropriate, employers or fellow employees.

• Limit the intervention to about 60 to 90 minutes. At longer sessions, anger may flare up and compassion tends to decline.

• Schedule a chemical dependency evaluation to follow the meeting.

Alive & Free, Hazelden newsletter, Hazelden Foundation.

likely to become alcoholic or drug dependent.

People often drink or use other drugs to avoid things that bother them—pressure from friends, stress in the family, hassles, the feeling that adults are on their case, the lousy feeling that they're different from everyone else in the world. They use these substances just to feel better. The problem is, drinking or using other drugs eventually makes things worse because all you care about is getting high, and once you start it's hard to stop; you need to use more just to feel normal. Alcohol and other substances change the way you think, and you start to believe things are better or worse than they really are. Alcohol and other drugs may make you feel good when you're high, but when they wear off, depression sets in.

Why is it so hard for individuals to get help for themselves?

It's tough for most people to admit that they have a serious substance abuse problem. It's especially hard to admit it when you're young because you think that kind of thing could never happen to you. Many people believe that alcoholics and other drug addicts are old people, or are street people, when, in reality, they can be anyone. People who have a serious problem with drinking or using other drugs might say that they are not using that much and that they won't get addicted. Denying that there's a problem is very common.

> Its tough for most people to admit that they have a serious substance abuse problem.

In fact, this denial, along with hiding the substance abuse from friends, becomes almost as big a problem as the drinking or other drug use itself. Becoming dependent on alcohol or other drugs makes you want to cut off the people who care about you, and you can end up feeling lonely and afraid.

To avoid being found out, serious problem drinkers and other drug users often spend more and more time alone, and think they can solve their problem all by themselves, or that a boyfriend or girlfriend can solve it for them. Getting better doesn't work that way. What has to happen is that your friend has to admit that alcohol and/or other drugs are messing up his or her life. However, you can help even if your friend does not admit to having a problem.

What can I do to help my friend?

It is possible for you to help a friend who is in serious trouble with alcohol or other drugs. Whether or not your friend takes your advice and gets help is really your friend's decision and responsibility. Sometimes, approaching the friend in trouble with another mutual friend can make our intervention easier since there is safety and support in numbers.

The first step in getting help is for your friend to talk to someone about his or her alcohol and drug use. Eventually, your friend will need to admit that there is a problem, and to agree to stop drinking and/or using other drugs completely. Your friend needs support and understanding, and someone he or she can trust to talk to about the problem. You can't force a friend to get help, but you can encourage and support your friend to seek and find professional help.

If you are worried about a friend, it is important for you to speak to someone in private who is knowledgeable and reassuring. Telling someone isn't being disloyal to your friend. It's important to know the facts about what's happening to your friend if you plan to help. Don't try to help your friend on your own until you have talked to someone you can trust—a counselor, teacher, doctor, nurse, parent, or someone at your church or synagogue. Ask this person to keep the conversation confidential. You don't have to mention your friend by name; you can just talk generally about the problem. Talking to a professional will help you figure out what the best steps are for you to take.

Guidelines for Helping

If you decide to speak to your friend, here are some guidelines that you and your advisor should consider in planning how and what you could do to help:

- Make sure the timing is right. Talk to your friend when he or she is sober or straight—before school is a good time.
- Never accuse your friend of being an alcoholic or a drug addict, but do express your concern. Try not to blame your friend for the problem; if you do, he or she might be turned off right away.
- Talk about your feelings. Tell your friend you're worried, and how it feels for you to see him or her drunk or high on other drugs.
- Tell your friend what you've seen him or her do when drinking or using other drugs. Give specific examples. Tell your friend you want to help.
- Speak in a caring and understanding tone of voice, not with pity but with friendship.
- Be prepared for denial and anger. Your friend may say there is nothing wrong and may get mad at you. Many people with alcohol and other drug problems react this way. When confronted, many users will defend their use, blame others for the problem, or give excuses for why they drink or use other drugs.
- Find out where help is available. You could offer to go with your friend to get help, but be prepared to follow through. This gesture will show your friend that you really care.
- You need to tell your friend that you are worried about him or her, and that someone who can help needs to be told. Your friend might get really mad at you, but if you say nothing, things may get worse and your friend may be in more danger.
- Your friend's problem is probably hard on you, too. The situation may have left you feeling lonely and afraid. Maybe you've thought, "What if I get my friend in trouble? What if I lose my friend over this? What if I don't do anything and something awful happens?" It's hard to keep all of these

questions and feelings to yourself. It's important that you talk about them. You can share these feelings with the person that you go to for help about your friend's problem. There are also support groups for people like you who are trying to help a friend, such as AL-Anon or Alateen, where you can learn more about people's alcohol and other drug use problems. Your school may have a substance abuse prevention counselor as well. . . .

What does my friend have to do to get help?

Probably the hardest decision your friend will be faced with is admitting that he or she has a problem. To get better and recover, your friend has to get some help to stop drinking or using other drugs.

Facing such a problem and asking for help can be a scary thing to do. Your friend will have to take an honest look at where drinking or other drug use has brought him or her, and admit that it has caused emotional and maybe physical pain. Your friend will have to see that it has robbed him or her of real friends, creativity, happiness, spirit, the respect of others, and even self-respect, and that it keeps your friend from growing up.

Your friend will not be able to solve this problem alone. He or she will need experienced help. A good counselor will support your friend and direct him or her to the kind of treatment and/or support groups that are most helpful.

Encourage your friend to talk to other people with drinking and other drug problems who are now in recovery, such as members of Alcoholics Anonymous (AA) and Narcotics Anonymous (NA). These groups are confidential, self-help

> Don't try to help your friend on your own until you have talked to someone you can trust.

organizations that offer assistance to anyone who has a drinking or other drug problem and wants to do something about it. AA and NA members are recovering alcoholics and addicts, so they have a special understanding of each other. Talking with others who have experienced similar problems is an important part of recovery. New members are encouraged to stay away from alcohol or other drugs "one day at a time." There is no fee for membership in these organizations. If your friend is afraid to go to a meeting alone, you can go along with him or her to an "open" meeting. Friends and family members are welcome to attend this type of meeting, and there are special meetings in most neighborhoods or communities. Local branches of AA and NA are listed in your phone directory.

> The potential consequences to your friend's life can be too severe to do nothing.

If your friend has a drinking or other drug problem, you may be the only one willing to reach out and help. Your friend may not appreciate your help right away, or he or she may realize it means you really care. Ultimately, it's up to your friend to get help. It is not your responsibility to make that happen. In fact, you can't make that happen. All you can do is talk to your friend, show how much you care, and encourage him or her to get help. Your concern and support might be just what is needed to help your friend turn his or her life around.

However, if your friend is in serious trouble with alcohol or other drugs, and you have been unable to get your friend to get help on his or her own, you should consider speaking with your friend's parents or guardian. The potential consequences to your friend's life can be too severe to do nothing.

A Letter to Children of Alcoholic Parents

An Adult Child of an Alcoholic

Many teenagers are exposed to alcoholism through their parents. In an open letter to such children and teens, a person who was raised by an alcoholic parent writes that they are not alone. Many people share their situation, the author writes, and children should not blame themselves for their parents' drinking problems. People in such situations should talk about it with someone they trust or check out Alateen group meetings.

Hello:

I'll bet you feel all alone when your mom or dad drinks too much, because maybe you think that no one else's mom or dad drinks like yours. Or maybe you think that no one knows how you feel. Do you know that there are plenty of kids your age who feel exactly like you, because their parents drink too much? I know how you feel, because one of my parents is an alcoholic too.

Feeling Alone

It's not easy. When I was your age, I felt so alone. Every time my parent started drinking, I had that funny feeling in my stom-

Excerpted from "An Adult Child of an Alcoholic," by the National Association for Children of Alcoholics (www.nacoa.org). Reprinted with permission.

ach that something wasn't right. I was scared to tell anyone. I wondered why I had a parent who drank so much.

I always wondered if I did anything to make my parent drink. None of my friends could spend the night at my house because I never knew when it would start. I didn't want my friends to know what went on in my house; besides, when my parent started to drink I never knew what would happen. I didn't want anyone to know what a mess it was when the drinking started. I felt ashamed, and believed my house was REALLY different from everybody else's.

When I grew up I moved away from my confusing house, and I began to meet other people who had alcoholic parents. I talked a lot to these people about how it was in my house, and I didn't feel embarrassed because they talked about what went on in their houses when their parents started drinking. I realized that other people had the same kinds of confusing things happen to them. Some people came from homes that were more messed up than mine, and other people came from homes that didn't have as many problems as mine did. But I realized one thing: that all the time when I was a kid, when I thought I was alone and the only one with parents who drank too much, I WASN'T.

> You aren't the only one with parents who drink too much. There are a lot of us here.

You aren't the only one with parents who drink too much. There are a lot of us here.

But now, I want to tell you some things about alcoholism that I wish someone had told me when I was a kid. Maybe these things will help you understand a little bit better, and maybe you won't blame yourself the next time your parents drink too much.

Four Facts

Fact #1. Alcoholism is a disease. Your parent is not a bad person; he or she has a disease that makes him or her lose control when

Important Facts About Children of Alcoholics

1. Alcoholism affects the entire family.

- Living with a non-recovering alcoholic in the family can contribute to stress for all members of the family. Each member may be affected differently. Not all alcoholic families experience or react to this stress in the same way. The level of dysfunction or resiliency of the non-alcoholic spouse is a key factor in the effects of problems impacting children.
- Children raised in alcoholic families have different life experiences than children raised in non-alcoholic families. Children raised in other types of dysfunctional families may have similar developmental losses and stressors as do children raised in alcoholic families.
- Children living with a non-recovering alcoholic score lower on measures of family cohesion, intellectual-cultural orientation, active-recreational orientation, and independence. They also usually experience higher levels of conflict within the family.
- Many children of alcoholics (COAs) experience other family members as distant and non-communicative.
- Children of alcoholics may be hampered by their inability to grow in developmentally healthy ways.

2. Many people report being exposed to alcoholism in their families.

- Seventy six million Americans, about 43% of the U.S. adult population, have been exposed to alcoholism in the family.
- Almost one in five adult Americans (18%) lived with an alcoholic while growing up.
- Roughly one in eight American adult drinkers is alcoholic or experiences problems due to the use of alcohol. The cost to society is estimated at in excess of $166 billion each year.
- There are an estimated 26.8 million COAs in the United States. Preliminary research suggests that over 11 million are under the age of 18.

National Clearinghouse for Alcohol and Drug Information.

drinking. Alcohol does that; when you drink too much, you do and say things that you normally wouldn't. Maybe the disease makes them do mean or stupid things that they would not do if they didn't drink.

Fact #2. You cannot control your parent's drinking. It is not your fault. Don't hide the bottle or try to be perfect; you can't do anything about your parent's drinking. You are not the reason why your parent drinks. You did not cause the disease.

Fact #3. You are not alone. There are lots of kids just like you. I'll bet there are some in your class at school—kids you would never think of might have a parent who drinks like yours. Maybe you know some of them because you've seen what goes on in their house. In fact, from all the surveys done in the United States, we know that there are about eleven million children with alcoholic parents living in our country. You really aren't alone.

Fact #4. You CAN talk about the problem. Find someone you trust who will talk to you. It could be a teacher, a friend's parent, a big brother or sister, or someone else who will listen to you. These are the "safe people" in your life. . . . Also, there is a group for kids called "Alateen." This group has meetings, like a club, and the kids there share tips on how to make their lives easier. Some schools have Alateen meetings on the school grounds during the day or after school. Maybe your teacher could help you find one. Or, you could look for the phone number of Alateen in the phone book or call directory assistance and ask for the number. (Sometimes you need to call Al-Anon or Alcoholics Anonymous to find Alateen meetings in your area.) Maybe a grown up you can trust will help you get to a meeting if transportation is a problem for you.

Please don't forget these four facts. They come in handy when you least suspect it.

Your Friend,
An adult child of an alcoholic

My Father the Alcoholic

Jenna Teter

Having an alcoholic parent can be very traumatic for children and teens, as the following story attests. The author, a seventeen-year-old high school student, describes the travails and embarrassments of having a father who is an alcoholic and a mother who pretends that nothing is wrong. She is persevering with the support of her boyfriend and through meeting other teenagers who come from alcoholic families.

"Don't worry," my mom said. "It'll be OK." Yeah, right. I knew better. It wouldn't be OK; it would be a football field away from OK. See, I'd heard it a zillion times before. "He won't drink tonight," Mom always said. Then Dad would come home from work, and we would hold our breath until we heard it: the pop of a beer can. That's the sound of my dad taking his first step on the downhill slide to Blottoville. So when my mom got it in her head that it was time she and Dad met my boyfriend, Teddy, I said, "No way."

"Jenna, you can't hide your family forever," Mom said.

Jekyll and Hyde Syndrome

That's exactly what I wanted to do, pretend I didn't live with a big, fat family secret: My dad is a drunk. He's also a great guy.

Reprinted from Jenna Teter, "My Father Is an Alcoholic," *Teen*, August 1997. Reprinted with permission from *Teen*.

Talk about Jekyll and Hyde.

There are times when he's just the coolest. Like one Halloween, he built a vine-covered swing inside our house and dressed up as Tarzan, swooping down on trick-or-treaters with a mega yell. But then the Hyde part comes out—and it's been coming out as long as I can remember. Once, when I was about 5, a loud thud awoke me in the middle of the night. I ran to the stairs. There, at the bottom, was Dad. He'd fallen and passed out. My mother was fretting over him, trying to rouse him. Though I couldn't understand then, now I know why she didn't call an ambulance right away—she was trying to come up with a cover story. She finally did call, and Dad was taken to the hospital with a broken nose. The next day, I heard the first of many lies from my mom's mouth as she called my dad's boss and explained his absence.

> The scariest part about living with my dad is never knowing what he's going to do.

I used to ask her what was wrong with Daddy, why he would be asleep in the den in the middle of the afternoon, why he always yelled and fell down at night. She always had an excuse, but I'm no idiot—it didn't take too long before I realized what made him "sick."

False Promises, Fearful Times

Once Mom figured out I knew about Dad's drinking, she started in with her false promises. I bought her lines—or tried to—until my 11th birthday. There was a party after school. I had a pretty new dress, a dining room full of friends, cake, the works. Mom swore Dad wouldn't interfere—I guess she set him up with a vodka bottle, thinking that would hold him. But no. He'd polished it off, then tried to get to the kitchen through the dining room. "No, Honey!" Mom shouted nervously. "It's just us girls! No boys allowed!" Dad burst in anyway, looking like a mess—hair wild, face red. He was loud and couldn't walk very well, and the more my mom fussed, the more he got irritated; he started to scream about the "stupid little brats" that had taken over his home. My friends were scared. My party was over. That was the last time I ever invited anyone to my house. But when my mom kept on about meeting Teddy, I finally gave in. "We'll have a barbecue!" she squealed.

From Dream Day to Nightmare

I felt really lucky to have found Teddy. He didn't care that I'm known as a nerd at school because I don't socialize much and won't hang with people who drink alcohol. I'm 17 now, and I have never had so much as a sip—drinking terrifies me. I gave in to my mom's pestering because, well, I just couldn't tell Teddy the truth, and he was getting suspicious. Like, "Why don't we ever study at your house?"

He was to come by on a Sunday. In the morning, I was nervous. But Dad was cool. Stone-cold sober. He helped me and Mom get everything ready. He was the dad I adored. By the time Teddy arrived, I was actually wondering what I'd been so worried about. My dad and Teddy tossed the Frisbee out on the lawn. Mom flashed the "thumbs up" sign. For a few glorious hours I was smiling, inside and out. I felt like there was nothing to feel ashamed about anymore. Toward the end of the day, Teddy took my hand and we walked to a nearby park and watched the sun set. I was so happy.

Spilling the Secret

When we got back, the second I walked through the door, I knew. The air was different—it seemed heavy somehow.

"Jenna?" my dad called loudly from the den. "Ted?"

"What's up?" Teddy asked.

What could I say? The scariest part about living with my dad is never knowing what he's going to do, when he's going to blow.

"Get in here!" he bellowed. "Both of you!"

What could I do? He's my dad. I led Teddy into the den.

"Who do you think you are?" my dad began, his words all slurring together. The top button of his pants was undone, his shirt untucked. An almost empty bottle and several beer cans stood beside him. "You think you know everything," he said. "You don't know squat."

Teddy looked at me, but I kept my face completely blank so I wouldn't set Dad off.

"Dad," I said softly. "Teddy has to get home."

"A man can't have a beer on a Sunday in his own home?!" (Obviously, he'd already been at it with Mom.)

"Dad . . ."

"Shut up!" he hollered, spit flying from his mouth. "I'm talking. Sit down!"

> My dad may still be drinking, and my mom may still be pretending, but I've got to find a way to deal.

Teddy and I sat down. I bit the inside of my mouth so I wouldn't cry. My mom poked her head through the door, but it only made him madder.

"Get out!" he shouted at her. Then he stood, stumbled toward the door and slammed it in her face. The force of it knocked him back onto the couch. Teddy scrambled to help. How could he know that was the worst thing to do?

"You think you're better than me?" Dad spat. The rims of his eyes were now bright red. I grabbed Teddy's sleeve.

"Leave him alone," I whispered. Big mistake.

"What the hell did you say?" my dad demanded.

"Daddy . . ."

"What . . . did . . . you . . . say?"

"I told him to leave you alo . . ." But before I could finish, he flung a magazine across the room and hit me in the neck. Then he started yelling about disrespect, and Teddy rushed over to make sure I wasn't hurt. It was surreal. I remember my ears ringing, but I think it was more about humiliation than pain. I hung my head and cried. Disgusted, my dad lurched out of the room. There was no hiding anymore.

No More Hiding

But Teddy dug deep and stood by me. Good thing. See, for the longest time, I'd faced the world as if I really came from a normal family with no problems. But Teddy knew the truth, and he didn't abandon me. He stayed, and that made me think maybe I didn't have to pretend anymore, that maybe it would be better if I let it all out.

I recently found a program to help teenagers who live with alcoholics. My dad may still be drinking, and my mom may still be pretending, but I've got to find a way to deal. Teddy's great, but through this program I've met other teens who are going through the same thing. I've only been to a couple of meetings so far, and I haven't had the nerve yet to get up and share my experiences out loud (writing them down, however, has been such a release!). But one thing I know for sure is I, for one, am getting help.

Chapter 5

Deciding About Alcohol

Can Alcohol Make You More Popular and Happy?

Teen Advice Online

Getting drunk is fun, writes a teenage boy to an Internet advice forum. At least that's how it seems with his friends. Why not try it? There are many reasons against using alcohol, three volunteer counselors in their teens and early twenties write back in response. Alcohol is a drug that must be treated with caution. Teen Advice Online consists of volunteers ages 13 and up who provide advice on teen issues.

I've grown up in a family who never smokes or drinks. Lately I've realized, what the hell is so bad about drinking? I have had a friend who got drunk off her ass, and threw up a little, but after that she got all the sympathy in the world by everyone. Now she is really popular and liked aside from her doing that. Since I'm sorta an outcast who wants to be noticed, i figure why the hell just not get a 6 pack and drink it all? I'm always sick of this shit about "oh, your too young" and "it is not healthy for you", but im in such a state of depression where nothing seems to fucking matter any more. I know lots of people who drink at the age of 14. I can understand how smoking gives you cancer

Excerpted from "Fun to Be Dizzy, Disoriented, and Drunk," by Teen Advice Online (www.teenadviceonline.org). Reprinted with permission.

and lung problems, and drugs just totally fuck you up, but i never see much about what alcohol does to you? In fact, it seems kinda fun to get all dizzy, disoriented, and drunk off your ass. so tell me, what is all the hype about not drinking beer. Why the hell not?

male 14 yrs.

USA

Laura's Answer

well, you're not alone in your desire to drink. it's estimated that 92% of teenagers have tried alcohol. in the US, over 100,000 people will die a year from alcohol (and i'm not talking about motor vehicle accidents). so no, "dizziness and disorientation" aren't the only things that can happen. everyone reacts differently to alcohol. your friend threw up, while others get aggressive and angry, threatening to hurt other people (some actually going through with the act). your reason for wanting to drink is the most worrisome thing that you have told me. to drink out of peer pressure, the need to fit in or to "have fun," are not acceptable for teenagers, but to drink because you're depressed can lead to SEVERE consequences. i'm sure you're well aware of what an alcoholic is, right? that's a person who needs to drink, who is so dependent on alcohol that she/he must have it or can possibly become suicidal, dangerous, hostile or severely depressed. depression is one of the LEADING factors which causes alcoholism,

> I know lots of people who drink at the age of 14.

and while there have been studies to prove that it's genetic, there is a lot of controversy surround the issue. to drink to "escape" your problems, to give you a temporary "high" will do nothing but depress you even more. the after effects of alcohol will actually make you feel even more low than you did before. . . .

if you don't want to feel so depressed, there are many things that you can do. i am not suggesting that you steer clear of al-

Monthly Drinking Among Students

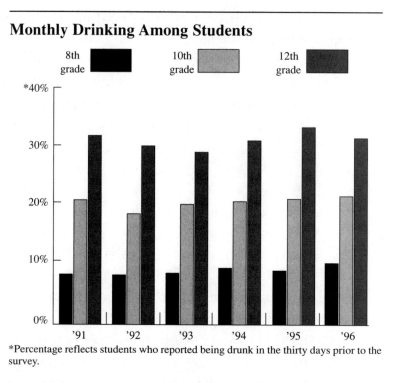

*Percentage reflects students who reported being drunk in the thirty days prior to the survey.

Source: The Monitoring the Future Study, the University of Michigan.

cohol for your entire life, not at all. but for one, you're a minor, and for two, you want to drink for the wrong reasons. . . .

Jenee's Answer

Okay, you wanted to know what is so bad about getting drunk and wasted I think I'm a perfect person to tell you. I spent a good chunk of my life getting totally wasted every weekend and a lot of week nights. It started off as just a party thing and then became something I had to do. There are no words I could use to describe the horror of waking up and not knowing where you are or where you've been. Or realizing you didn't just put your own life in jeopardy you also put the lives of everyone you pass along the way home. I could tell you my worst drunk stories (like the time I drank till I threw up blood, or how I lost two friends to drunk driving) but I'm going to spare you. I hope you realize what the big deal about drinking is, if not I'd be more than happy to tell you some more stories.

Rachel's Answer

It's fun to be dizzy, disoriented, and drunk? Hmmm . . . what about the next morning? When you wake up with a killer headache, feeling like . . . well, you can guess probably from hearing people talk about it . . . and let me tell you, it isn't pretty. Is it worth it? I don't know. Some people say yes, some people say no. Does it give you instant popularity? Well, my status at school upped for a little bit after I showed up at some of the drinking parties, but was it for the right reasons? I don't know. We had a common bond . . . our puking. But then later I went to a party as a designated driver. Had a blast . . . I didn't drink . . . I didn't need to.

The bottom line? Drinking isn't all it's cracked up to be. Some people like it, but I guess those people are always going to be there. It's something that a lot of people get dependent on. I don't think I need that in my life. I don't think you really need that either, but I guess it's up to you.

Fighting Peer Pressure

Valerie Banner

Valerie Banner, a college student and reporter for *Teen People,* writes that she did not drink while in high school and tried beer only once in college. The key to avoiding alcohol was her friends who stuck together and did not drink. People are now surprised when she tells them she's never been drunk, but do not pressure her to drink. To her, there are far better ways than drinking to have a good time.

I didn't drink when I was in high school. My parents discouraged it, but more important, my friends didn't drink. We stuck together at parties, which made it easy to "just say no." Last summer, we talked about what would happen when we went to separate colleges in the fall. We knew the drinking scene would be different and we wouldn't be able to be there for each other all the time.

For me, things changed very little. I made new friends at college who share my stance on drinking. But one old friend started ed sending me e-mails from her school about all the fun we had missed by not drinking sooner. She talked about how high her tolerance for alcohol was getting. I worried about her going from one extreme to the other. Still, hearing her tell me how great it was piqued my curiosity. One weekend, a friend from home had a few people over and offered me a beer. I was curi-

Reprinted from Valerie Banner, "Fighting Peer Pressure," *Teen People*, March 2000. Reprinted with permission from *Teen People*.

ous, so I tried it for the first time. It tasted bad, and it made me feel lightheaded, but mostly tired. I haven't tried it again.

No Pressure

Most people are surprised to learn I've never been drunk, but they don't pressure me to drink after I say no. A lot of people have even said they think it's cool, and that they admire my strong will. I want to have fun, but I think there are better ways to do it than throwing up in the cool mist of the toilet bowl. That's how one friend of mine spent last Saturday night. The next day, he had a throbbing headache. He didn't remember anything that had happened. And he'll probably do it all again next weekend.

> I want to have fun, but I think there are better ways to do it than throwing up in the cool mist of the toilet bowl.

My night was different, although I also went to a party where most people were drinking. It was fun at first. My friends and I circled the room talking and laughing with all the people we knew. But drunk people aren't funny for very long. As the night wore on, we got tired of supporting people who couldn't walk straight and avoiding puddles of puke. So we left early, ordered pizza and had our own party.

Making Responsible Decisions About Alcohol

Elizabeth A. Ryan

Whether and how to drink alcohol are questions that you will face your whole life, writes Elizabeth A. Ryan, the author of *Straight Talk About Drugs and Alcohol.* The decisions people make vary widely, but the bottom line for teens should be to maintain their power of choice, and not lose it to addiction, peer pressure, or other causes. Ryan lists questions people can ask themselves to determine whether their relationship with alcohol has turned harmful, suggestions for healthy drinking, and tips on saying "no" to a drink.

Whether or not you want to drink, how much, and in what circumstances, are questions that you will be facing throughout your whole life. The answers to these questions will be different for everybody. Some people may discover that they don't like alcohol at all. Or they may consider that drinking is morally wrong. Or they may discover that their allergy or potential dependence on alcohol is so great that even one drink is too many.

Other people may decide that they enjoy drinking, and that they can find comfortable ways to make drinking a part of their lives. They will know how to tell the difference between drinking that is enjoyable and drinking that is the only way they know how to have fun; drinking that helps them unwind once in a while and drinking that is absolutely necessary for their well-being. They will understand that there are situations in which drinking is inappropriate or dangerous—such as before driving or during pregnancy. They will also know how to monitor their own drinking, to discover if they are using alcohol in a way that covers up other problems or feelings that might be better faced head-on.

Whatever you decide about drinking, remember that it is your power of choice that is the most important. You want to make decisions that increase your control over your life, rather than take that control away. . . .

When Is Drinking a "Problem"?

Because drinking is so common in our society, it's often difficult to distinguish between "problem" and "social" drinking. The questionnaires that follow are designed to help you think about the way you use alcohol. There are no right and wrong answers to any of the questions. But if you find yourself answering yes to a question, stop a minute and think about it. Let yourself react honestly to the feelings that the question provokes. Are you exhibiting a type of behavior that you are happy with? Had you realized that this was what you were doing? Is it difficult for you to admit the part alcohol plays in your life? If you find yourself answering "yes" to several of these questions, you may decide that you have a problem with drinking. Even if this problem only surfaces at particular times—on weekends, at parties, when you're having trouble with some particular aspect of your

> Whatever you decide about drinking, remember that it is your power of choice that is the most important.

life—it's still a problem. Alcohol may be covering up your feelings or keeping you from facing a situation head-on, even if you are still able to function in your daily life. Think, then, about whether you want to change your relationship with alcohol.

1. Do you find yourself getting really drunk a lot?
2. Does your personality change when you're drinking? Do you pick fights, come on very strong with people you're interested in, say outrageous things, or otherwise behave in a way that you wouldn't if you were sober?
3. Do you find yourself having all kinds of accidents?
4. Are people around you starting to express concern, either with your drinking or with your general appearance, behavior, performance in school, etcetera?
5. Do you feel you need alcohol to go through with something difficult, like a date? Do you drink *in order* to have a good time, rather than as *part* of a good time?
6. Do you hide drinks? Do you plan ahead when and where you're going to *drink next?*
7. Do you feel guilty about drinking?
8. Are you unable to discuss your drinking with anyone?
9. Do you sometimes forget what you did during whole periods of time when you were drunk?
10. Do you think and talk about drinking often?
11. Do you drink now more than you used to?
12. Do you sometimes gulp drinks?
13. Do you often take a drink to help you relax? Do you feel that you *can't* relax without a drink, or that you usually can't?
14. Do you drink when you are alone?
15. Do you keep a bottle hidden somewhere—at home or at school—for a quick pick-me-up? Does the thought of not knowing where you could get a drink if you needed one make you feel panicky?
16. Do you ever start drinking without really thinking about it?

17. Do you drink in the mornings to relieve a hangover?

18. Have you ever been arrested for an alcohol-related charge?

19. Have you ever missed school or work because of drinking? Because of a hangover? Because of being wiped out after a wild party or a night of drinking with a friend?

20. Do you dislike this quiz because it hits too close to home?

If you find yourself going through elaborate rituals to prevent a hangover, this might be a sign that you are drinking in a way that threatens to disrupt your life.

If any of these questions makes you nervous, or if answering these questions has made you want to think more about your use of alcohol, you may want to contact some of the organizations listed in the appendix.* Your school counselor, a private therapist, or a local organization may also offer help in thinking about this issue, as well as reassurance that you are not alone.

Suggestions for Healthy Drinking

If you are still comfortable with the idea of drinking but want to think about ways to do so in a more healthy manner, you might want to take some of the following suggestions:

- Set your own limit, based on alcohol's effect on your personal health and fitness goals. If you're going to a party or dinner with friends, decide how much is too much ahead of time, and stick to your limit.
- Have something to eat. Even if you can't eat a whole meal, eat something—especially a protein and a fat. A glass of milk, a piece of cheese, or some bread and butter will help soften alcohol's effect on your system.
- Sip drinks, don't gulp them. This will help you stay aware of how much you are drinking, and will make it easier to drink less over the course of an evening.

*Editor's note: A listing of organizations can be found on pp. 135–39.

- Dilute your drink. A mixed drink is easier on your system than a straight shot of liquor. Wine is easier still. And beer is probably the best choice for someone trying to cut down on drinking, because beer fills you up more quickly than other kinds of alcohol. (That doesn't mean you should cut back on one type of liquor by increasing your beer drinking, however!)
- Don't drink to elevate your mood—to relieve feelings of anxiety, pain, or depression. Since alcohol is a depressant, it tends to perpetuate your mood, and can actually make bad feelings worse.
- Don't drink to signals, such as every Friday night, every big date, just before you go to bed to help you sleep, etcetera. If you can't imagine not drinking on a social occasion try it and see what happens.
- One or fewer drinks per hour will help prevent hangovers. It's drinking a lot in a short time that makes hangovers worse. Alcohol dehydrates you and makes it difficult to ab-

Annual Costs of Alcohol Use by Youth

(Total = $58.38 Billion, in 1998 Dollars)

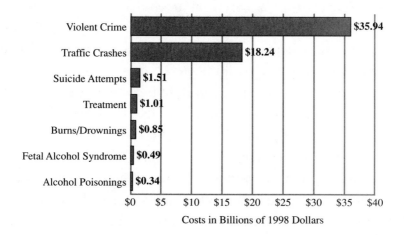

CSAT by Fax, October 27, 1999. Center for Substance Abuse Treatment.

sorb vitamins. (If you find yourself going through elaborate rituals to prevent a hangover, this might be a sign that you are drinking in a way that threatens to disrupt your life.)

- Sprees or binges, where you drink a lot in a short period, are worse for your health than drinking a little at a time, so stay aware of your drinking patterns.

> You might want some ideas for how to refuse alcohol when it is offered to you.

- Of course, you should never drink and drive. And never ride in a car driven by someone who has been drinking. Decide at the beginning of the evening how you will handle transportation: by having one of the group stay sober, by chipping in for a taxi, by arranging for someone else who is sober to pick you up, by using public transportation, by spending the night at the place you drink.

- Don't match other people's drinking. Different people have different body weights, different sensitivities to liquor, different emotional reactions, and so on. Women have less efficient livers than men, and usually have lower body weights, so they should not try to match men's drinking.

How to Say No

Finally, having read this material or having already made your decision, you may want to work on your ability to say "no" to a drink. Whether this means cutting out alcohol completely, or just stopping at the point that feels right for you, you might want some ideas for how to refuse alcohol when it is offered to you. These phrases might be helpful:

- "No thanks, I'm driving."
- "No, thanks, I don't want to get into trouble with my parents (teachers, friends, grandparents, etcetera)."
- "No, thanks, if I drink I'll lose my privileges (such as the use of the car)."
- "No, thanks, I don't like the taste."

- "No, thanks, I don't drink."
- "No, thanks, it's just not me."
- "No, thanks, I've got to study later (or pick up a friend, or get up early, etcetera)."
- "No, thanks, I've got a big day tomorrow (or a big game, or some other important activity coming up)."
- "No, thanks, I want to keep a clear head."
- "No, thanks, I usually end up embarrassing myself."
- "No, thanks, drinking makes me tired."
- "No, thanks, I'm on a diet."
- "No, thanks, I'm in training."
- "No, thanks, what else have you got?"
- "No, thanks.". . .

Bibliography

Books

Nathan Aaseng — *Teens and Drunk Driving*. San Diego: Lucent, 2000.

Eleanor Ayer — *It's OK to Say No: Choosing Sexual Abstinence*. New York: Rosen, 1997.

Paul Dolmetsch, ed. — *Teens Talk About Alcohol and Alcoholism*. Garden City, NY: Doubleday, 1987.

Margaret O. Hyde and John F. Setaro — *Alcohol 101: An Overview for Teens*. Brookfield, CT: Twenty-First Century, 1999.

Jean McBee Knox — *Drinking, Driving, and Drugs*. New York: Chelsea House, 1988.

Elaine Landau — *Teenage Drinking*. Hillside, NJ: Enslow, 1994.

Evelyn Leite — *Different Like Me: A Book for Teens Who Worry About Their Parent's Use of Alcohol/Drugs*. Minneapolis, MN: Johnson Institute, 1987.

Jane Claypool Miner — *Alcohol and You*. 3rd ed. New York: Franklin Watts, 1997.

Hayley R. Mitchell   *Teen Alcoholism*. San Diego: Lucent, 1998.

Judy Monroe   *Alcohol*. Hillside, NJ: Enslow, 1994.

Marc Alan Schuckit   *Educating Yourself About Alcohol and Drugs: A People's Primer*. New York: Plenum Press, 1995.

Nancy Shuker   *Everything You Need to Know About an Alcoholic Parent*. New York: Rosen, 1990.

Richard Steins   *Alcohol Abuse: Is This Danger on the Rise?* Brookfield, CT: Twenty-First Century, 1995.

Periodicals

Brandy Allen   "I Started Drinking in the Third Grade," *Sassy*, October 1996.

Rebecca Barry   "Under the Influence," *Seventeen*, August 1996.

Jim Bernat   "My Boyfriend Was a Binge Drinker," *Teen Magazine*, December 1995.

Shanta M. Bryant   "Youth Warning Other Youth About Drugs and Alcohol," *Christian Social Action*, February 1998.

Joseph A. Califano   "The Least Among Us: Children of Substance-Abusing Parents," *America*, April 24, 1999.

Congressional Digest   "Zero Tolerance: Reducing Drinking and Driving by Young Drivers," June/July 1998.

Per Ola d'Aulaire   "I Can Quit Whenever I Want,"
and Emily d'Aulaire   *Reader's Digest*, June 1997.

Melanie Franklin   "My Daughter Was a Drunk Driver," *Good Housekeeping,* August 1998.

Larry Fritzlan   "Raising the Bottom," *Family Therapy Networker*, July 1999.

Laurel Graeber   "Stop Preteen Drinking Before It Starts," *Parents*, January 2000.

Tony Guy   "Undercover Teen: Busting the Bad Guys," *Teen Magazine*, March 1996.

Matthew J. Herper   "Binge and Purge," *Reason*, November 1999.

Jack Hitt   "The Battle of the Binge," *New York Times Magazine*, October 24, 1999.

Issues and   "Alcohol Issues," February 20, 1998.
Controversies On File

Journal of the   "Benefits and Dangers of Alcohol,"
American Medical   January 6, 1999.
Association

Joey Kennedy   "Drunk Driving Makes a Comeback," *Redbook*, May 19, 1997.

Kathiann M.   "The Dangers of Alcohol," *Current*
Kowalski   *Health,* February 1998.

David Leonhardt   "How Big Liquor Takes Aim at Teens,"
                      Business Week, May 19, 1997.

Melanie Mannarino   "Big Gulp," *Seventeen*, March 1998.

David L. Marcus   "Drinking to Get Drunk," *U.S. News &
                      World Report*, March 27, 2000.

Julie Monahan   "True Stories: Teens with Drinking
                      Problems," *Teen Magazine*, April 1993.

Maria Purdy   "Drinking Without Thinking," *Teen
                      Magazine*, May 1998.

Warren Richards   "I Drove Drunk," *Seventeen*, November
                      1993.

Andrea Rock   "The Binge Generation," *Ladies' Home
                      Journal,* December 1999.

Sabrina Rubin   "Binge Drinking, a Campus Killer,"
                      Reader's Digest, November 1998.

Cheryl Tevis   "Communities Wage War on Teen Sub-
                      stance Abuse," *Successful Farming*,
                      October 1999.

J.J. Thompson   "Plugging the Kegs," *U.S. News &
                      World Report*, January 26, 1998.

James Tobin   "Family Disease," *Parents*, September
                      1998.

Henry Wechsler   "Alcohol and the American College
                      Campus," *Change*, July/August 1996.

Organizations and Websites

The editors have compiled the following list of organizations concerned with the issues debated in this book. The descriptions are derived from materials provided by the organizations. All have publications or information available for interested readers. The list was compiled on the date of publication of the present volume; the information provided here may change. Be aware that many organizations take several weeks or longer to respond to inquiries, so allow as much time as possible.

Al-Anon Family Groups Headquarters

1600 Corporate Landing Pkwy., Virginia Beach, VA 23454-5617
(757) 563-1600 • fax: (757) 563-1655
e-mail: WSO@al-anon.org • website: www.al-anon.alateen.org

Al-Anon is a fellowship of men, women, and children whose lives have been affected by an alcoholic family member or friend. Members share their experience, strength, and hope to help each other and perhaps to aid in the recovery of the alcoholic. Al-Anon provides information on its local chapters and on its affiliated organization, Alateen. Its publications include the monthly magazine, *The Forum*, the semiannual *Al-Anon Speaks Out*, the bimonthly *Alateen Talk*, and several books and pamphlets.

Alcoholics Anonymous (AA)

Grand Central Station, PO Box 459, New York, NY 10163
(212) 870-3400 • fax: (212) 870-3003
website: www.aa.org

Alcoholics Anonymous is a worldwide fellowship of sober alcoholics, whose recovery is based on twelve steps. AA requires no dues or fees and accepts no outside funds. It is self-supporting through voluntary contributions of members. It is not affiliated with any other organization. AA's primary purpose is to carry the AA message to the alcoholic who still suffers. Its catalog of publications include the pamphlets *A Brief Guide to Alcoholics Anonymous*, *Young People and AA*, and *Is AA for You?*

Canadian Centre on Substance Abuse (CCSA)

75 Albert St., Suite 300, Ottawa, ON K1P 5E7 CANADA
(613) 235-4048 ext. 222 • fax: (613) 235-8108
e-mail: info@ccsa.ca • website: www.ccsa.ca

A Canadian clearinghouse on substance abuse, the CCSA works to disseminate information on the nature, extent, and consequences of substance abuse and to support and assist organizations involved in substance abuse treatment, prevention, and educational programming. The CCSA publishes several books, including *Canadian Profile: Alcohol, Tobacco, and Other Drugs*, as well as reports, policy documents, brochures, research papers, and the newsletter *Action News*.

Hazelden Institute

PO Box 176, 15251 Pleasant Valley Rd., Center City, MN 55012-9640
(800) 329-9000 • fax: (651) 213-4590
e-mail: info@hazelden.org • website: www.hazelden.org

Hazelden is a nonprofit organization dedicated to helping people recover from alcoholism and other addictions. It provides residential and outpatient treatment for adults and young people, programs for families affected by chemical dependency, and training for a variety of professionals. The institute publishes the quarterly newsletter *Hazelden Voice*, the bimonthly newspaper column *Alive & Free*, books, press releases, research reports, and public policy papers.

National Association for Children of Alcoholics (NACoA)

11426 Rockville Pike, Suite 100, Rockville, MD 20852
(888) 554-2627 • fax: (301) 468-0987
e-mail: nacoa@erols.com • website: www.health.org/nacoa

NACoA is the only national nonprofit membership organization working on behalf of children of alcoholics. Its mission is to advocate for all children and families affected by alcoholism and other drug dependencies. The association publishes books, pamphlets, videos, educational kits, and the bimonthly *NACoA Network Newsletter*.

National Clearinghouse for Alcohol and Drug Information (NCADI)

PO Box 2345, Rockville, MD 208487-2345
(800) 729-6686 • (301) 468-2600
TDD: (800) 487-4889 or (301) 230-2867 (hearing impaired)
e-mail: info@health.org • website: www.health.org

The NCADI is a federal government organization that provides free and low-cost information on alcoholism and other addictions, including material geared specifically for teens.

Students Against Destructive Decisions (SADD)

PO Box 800, Malboro, MA 01752
(800) 787-5777 • fax: (508) 481-5759
website: www.saddonline.com

This organization is aimed at teens and seeks to address the problems of impaired driving, underage drinking, and alcohol and drug abuse. It provides a support network for students to set up their own SADD chapters in schools.

Websites

Alcohol: Problems and Solutions Website
website: www2.potsdam.edu/alcohol-info

This website describes alcohol use and abuse along with effective ways to reduce or eliminate drinking problems such as underage drinking, drinking and driving, and binge drinking. The *In Their Own Words* section contains interviews with experts on a wide variety of alcohol-related issues, *In the News* provides current news articles for downloading, and *In My Opinion* offers essays including "It's Better to Teach Safe Use of Alcohol."

Another Empty Bottle
website: http://alcoholismhelp.com

Another Empty Bottle is a website for alcoholics and their friends and family. It includes the Alcoholism Index, a directory of alcohol-related Internet resources, chat rooms, and discussion areas. It also features "In Our Words," a collection of submitted personal stories on alcoholism.

Hope and Healing WebChronicles
website: www.hopeandhealing.com

Hope and Healing WebChronicles is an online resource focusing on spiritual and personal transformations for individuals and families suffering from alcoholism, alcohol abuse, addiction, and codependency. Its website includes interviews, columns, articles, and other information sources.

Lowe Family Foundation

website: www.lowefamily.org

The Lowe Family Foundation is a charity organization dedicated to providing H.E.L.P.—Healing, Educational, and Loving Programs—for people coping with alcohol abuse in their family. The website includes interviews with experts on alcohol abuse and a comprehensive listing of alcohol and drug abuse counseling organizations in twenty-eight states.

Teen Advice Online (TAO)

website: www.teenadviceonline.org

TAO's teen counselors from around the world offer advice for teens on substance abuse, as well as relationships, dating, sex, and other issues. Teens can submit questions to the counselors or read about similar problems in the archives.

Index